Plough Quarterly

BREAKING GROUND FOR A RENEWED

Winter 2019, Number 19

Artists: Margaret McWethy, Albrecht Dürer, Raphael, Gérard David, Jackie Morris, Gustaf Tenggren, Sergey Dushkin, Anja Percival, Dmitry Samofalov, Christoph Wetzel, Sherrie York, Cathleen Rehfield

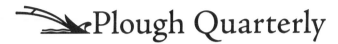

Plough Quarterly

WWW.PLOUGH.COM

Meet the community behind *Plough*

Plough Quarterly is published by the Bruderhof, an international community of families and singles seeking to follow Jesus together. Members of the Bruderhof are committed to a way of radical discipleship in the spirit of the Sermon on the Mount. Inspired by the first church in Jerusalem (Acts 2 and 4), they renounce private property and share everything in common in a life of nonviolence, justice, and service to neighbors near and far. The community includes people from a wide range of backgrounds. There are twenty-three Bruderhof settlements in both rural and urban locations in the United States, England, Germany, Australia, and Paraguay, with around 2,900 people in all.

To learn more or arrange a visit, see the community's website at *bruderhof.com.*

Plough Quarterly features original stories, ideas, and culture to inspire everyday faith and action. Starting from the conviction that the teachings and example of Jesus can transform and renew our world, we aim to apply them to all aspects of life, seeking common ground with all people of goodwill regardless of creed. The goal of *Plough Quarterly* is to build a living network of readers, contributors, and practitioners so that, in the words of Hebrews, we may "spur one another on toward love and good deeds."

Plough Quarterly includes contributions that we believe are worthy of our readers' consideration, whether or not we fully agree with them. Views expressed by contributors are their own and do not necessarily reflect the editorial position of *Plough* or of the Bruderhof communities.

Editors: Peter Mommsen, Veery Huleatt, Sam Hine. Creative Director: Clare Stober. Art director: Emily Alexander. Designer: Rosalind Thomson. Managing editor: Shana Goodwin. Contributing editors: Maureen Swinger, Susannah Black.

Founding Editor: Eberhard Arnold (1883–1935).

Plough Quarterly No. 19: School for Life

Published by Plough Publishing House, ISBN 978-0-87486-327-7

Copyright © 2019 by Plough Publishing House. All rights reserved.

Editorial Office	Subscriber Services	United Kingdom	Australia
PO Box 398	PO Box 345	Brightling Road	4188 Gwydir Highway
Walden, NY 12586	Congers, NY 10920-0345	Robertsbridge	Elsmore, NSW
T: 845.572.3455	T: 800.521.8011	TN32 5DR	2360 Australia
info@plough.com	subscriptions@plough.com	T: +44(0)1580.883.344	T: +61(0)2.6723.2213

Plough Quarterly (ISSN 2372-2584) is published quarterly by Plough Publishing House, PO Box 398, Walden, NY 12586.
Individual subscription $32 per year in the United States; Canada add $8, other countries add $16.
Periodicals postage paid at Walden, NY 12586 and at additional mailing offices.
POSTMASTER: Send address changes to *Plough Quarterly*, PO Box 345, Congers, NY 10920-0345.

STATEMENT OF OWNERSHIP, MANAGEMENT, AND CIRCULATION (Required by 39 U.S.C. 3685) 1. Title of publication: Plough Quarterly. 2. Publication No: 0001-6584. 3. Date of filing: September 28, 2018. 4. Frequency of issue: Quarterly. 5. Number of issues published annually: 4. 6. Annual subscription price: $32.00. 7. Complete mailing address of known office of publication: Plough Quarterly, P.O. Box 398, Walden, NY 12586. 8. Same. 9. Publisher: Plough Publishing House, same address. Editor: Peter Mommsen, same address. Managing Editor: Sam Hine, same address. 10. Owner: Plough Publishing House, P.o. Box 398, Walden, NY 12586. 11. Known bondholders, mortgages, and other securities: None. 12. The purpose, function, and nonprofit status of this organization and the exempt status for federal income tax purposes have not changed during preceding 12 months. 13. Publication Title: Plough Quarterly. 14. Issue date for circulation data below: Fall 2017–Summer 2018. 15. Extent and nature of circulation: Average No. copies of each issue during preceding 12 months: A. Total number of copies (net press run)—15,340. B.1. Mailed outside-county paid subscriptions: 9,778. B.2. Mailed in-county paid subscriptions: 0. B.3. Paid distribution outside the mails including sales through dealers and carriers, street vendors, counter sales, and other non-USPS paid distribution: 266. B.4. Other classes mailed through the USPS: 0. C. Total paid distribution: 10,044. D.1. Free distribution by mail: Outside-county—1,239. D.2. In-county—0. D3. Other classes mailed through the USPS—0. Free distribution outside the mail—59. E. Total free distribution: 1,298. F. Total Distribution: 11,342. G. Copies not distributed: 3,997. H. Total: 15,340. I. Percent paid—88.55%. Actual No. copies of single issue published nearest to filing date: A. 17,400. B.1. 10,355. B.2. 0. B.3. 335. B.4. 0. C. 10,690. D.1. 1,602. D.2. 0. D.4. 70. E. 1,672. F. 12,362. G. 5,038. H. 17,400. I. 86.47%. Electronic copy circulation: Average No. copies of each issue during preceding 12 months: A. Total No. Electronic Copies: 226. B. Total paid print copies plus paid electronic copies: 10,270. C. Total print distribution plus paid electronic copies: 11,569. D. Percent paid: 88.78%. Actual No. copies of single issue published nearest to filing date: A. 181. B. 10,871. C. 12,543. D. 86.67%. 17. Publication of Statement of Ownership: Winter 2019. 18. I certify that the statements made by me above are correct and complete. Sam Hine, Editor, September 28, 2018.

School for Life

PETER MOMMSEN

Dear Reader,

"WHAT'S THE POINT of school?" It's a question my son is doubtless the several-billionth schoolboy to ask when told to park his soccer ball and start his homework. There's a stock set of responses parents tend to repeat at such moments. But the question remains unsettled, even two centuries after the Prussians invented compulsory education.

Schools are a mirror of our society as a whole; what we want for schools makes plain what and whom we value in our common life. For example, the Prussian idea of what a school is for – to mold the populace to serve the state – seems foreign to today's liberal democracy. In vogue, instead, are slogans like *acquiring marketable skills* and *realizing your full potential.*

Such slogans reflect two main ideas. The first is that a school should prepare a child for the job market: the goal is "student achievement and preparation for global competitiveness," in the words of the US Department of Education. The second is that a school should aid a child to become a self-fulfilled individualist – a "leader and catalyst" who is "empowered" to "pursue your passion" (to pick a few common catch phrases from university brochures).

These ideas powerfully shape our culture, thanks not least to their influence in the Silicon Valley worldview we live and breathe. Both boil down, ultimately, to pursuing one supreme value: individual success in a competitive world. What's not said is that this kind of success comes at someone else's expense. By definition, not everyone can be above average. Despite its invocations of creativity and diversity, for much of humanity the creed of Tech Age meritocracy is a bleak and merciless one.

Fortunately, these aren't the only ideas out there, as a rewarding new book by Alan Jacobs reminds us. In *The Year of Our Lord 1943* Jacobs describes how, during World War II, a network of Christian thinkers including Simone Weil, C. S. Lewis, and Jacques Maritain imagined what post-war society should look like. They focused especially on schools.

One of them, the poet W. H. Auden, was a schoolteacher himself. In his 1943 talk "Vocation and Society," he appealed to his fellow educators to focus on the spiritual element of education. This meant helping students discover their vocation – a life-defining task they know they must do, even at the cost of suffering. Most people, distracted by earning and spending, never find such a vocation. But educators, said Auden, must strive to "make a sense of vocation the normal instead of the exceptional thing."

In the Christian tradition, the life of discipleship is also a school. In this educational community, under the instruction of our one Teacher, we learn not to seek empowerment, but to find strength in weakness; not to out-achieve others, but to serve them; not to pursue our passion, but to obey a call. That, after all, is the message of Christ's incarnation as a vulnerable human baby, the great mystery we celebrate each year at Christmas.

Warm greetings,

Peter

Peter Mommsen

Editor

Healing, not Band-Aids, for Combat Veterans

On Scott Beauchamp's "Warriors on Stage," Autumn 2018: Beauchamp's critique of contemporary attempts at dealing with combat veterans' spiritual and psychological injuries rightly asks how effective these really are. Programs that stay within the bounds of secular therapy, he argues, are insufficient for addressing the damage suffered by warriors. As an example, he takes the Greek dramas staged by Theater of War Project, in which American veterans play parts written by an Athenian veteran. Originally religious, the Greek plays can't be used outside their religious context as technical fixes – even artistic technical fixes – of spiritual problems.

But productions of Sophocles' *Ajax* are not the only things that fail to take seriously the spiritual reality of the wounds of war. Military ministry – which is, or at least ought to be, at the frontlines of postbellum trauma treatment – itself frequently fails to meet this need for the transcendent. At least in my experience as an Air Force chaplain, military ministry often falls into the same trap that Beauchamp identifies. It sees itself more as a sort of spiritual Band-Aid, a therapeutic measure taken for the purpose of getting the troops "spiritually fit to fight," than as a source of genuine healing and redemption.

The problem is, of course, that the ordering principle for us chaplains is still the advance of the nation-state by violence. The human person is made an instrument for that end. Spirituality is ornamentation or tool. This framework, as Beauchamp suggests, cannot provide the transcendental vision necessary for the kind of healing required for the veteran's reintegration into society and eventual flourishing.

Chaplains must provide a counter-narrative, an eschatology that promises, in Christ, something more than the worldwide triumph of the secular nation-state. Only this can heal: this invitation into a form of life beyond the violence of the city of man. Chaplains and other ministers must, in short, be reminders of the holy. We must tell soldiers that they are not militarized instruments of the nation-state: they are children of God. Fair warning to my fellow chaplains: this might not (and probably won't) directly advance the mission, and might even prove disruptive or require self-sacrifice. Which is to say, it might require we be Christian.

Fr. Seth Snyder, Waterford, OH
Snyder is a military chaplain in the US Air Force Reserves.

Reckoning with Repentance

On Emily Hallock's "A Man of Honor," Autumn 2018: I will not be renewing my subscription to *Plough.* Emily Hallock's article in your last issue is a shameful and potentially harmful viewpoint. I pray no LGBTQ persons read this and feel their inherent self-worth and goodness demeaned.

The only glimmer of hope in this article is a call to be more welcoming to LGBTQ persons – but that is quickly soiled by referring to her father giving in to temptation, or a lesbian woman who was able to "renounce her . . . lifestyle." In a world that already subjects LGBTQ to significant abuse, the potential for further harm through a viewpoint like this is monumental. The LGBTQ suicide rate is significantly higher than that of straight people. And articles like Hallock's contribute to this. *Rev. Brian Chenowith, Lexington, KY*

Emily Hallock responds: I've received numerous responses since sharing my father's story, among them several like Brian Chenowith's. It goes without saying that I share

Chenowith's concern for vulnerable people. But can it really be true to claim, as he does, that the mere act of writing a true story such as my father's is "shameful" and "harmful"? As is clear from other responses I've received to the article, my father's experience, and ours as a family, is hardly unique.

There's an essential element of my father's story that Chenowith fails to reckon with. What made my beloved Dad feel remorse for his gay relationship, and then for the HIV infection that eventually took his life, was not society's judgment. It was the judgment of his own conscience: an inner sense of conviction for sin. When he repented, he was given a peace and a joy that he recognized as the fruit of being freed from an evil through God's forgiveness. His peace and joy were a blessing for our whole family, something I will always remember now that he is gone.

Yes, we need a lot more compassion for one another; Christians in particular must do far better here, as I write in my article. Such compassion cannot mean silencing those stories, like my Dad's, that may seem unsettling or controversial. Surely, true compassion includes respect for the dignity and inviolability of each person's conscience.

Seeing Everyday Beauty

On Roger Scruton's "The Beauty of Belonging," Autumn 2018: Reading Roger Scruton on matters of beauty is a pleasure, if something of a guilty one. At times he paints with a broad rhetorical brush, and I'm never quite sure if I've been carried away in metaphysical safety, or not. I'm a bit of a sucker for the praise of beauty, and so I remain susceptible. One strives, however, to be a *reformed* aesthete, with a Plato on the shoulder to remind one that the Beautiful and the Good don't always coincide.

I admire Scruton's attempt to join together what Hegel declared divorced forevermore, that is, art and religion. But it's easier to see the connection he makes between beauty and the sacred than to hear what he thinks beauty has to say in the tumble of the everyday. That's where his argument falters for me. I worry that his beauty seems at once too grand and not self-respecting enough: I'm not willing to concede that all buildings are shrines somehow, even if I agree that buildings do better with a shrine in

them. He wants it clear that beauty accommodates itself to the everyday; while the everyday, lacking beauty wholesale, requires beauty's abbreviation as awkward window dressing.

Heraclitus had an uphill battle when he refused to budge from the kitchen, inviting his foreign guests to come in, "for here there are gods also." But the missing piece is here somewhere: van Cleve's Mary is beautiful in her beautiful bedroom, but I fear for her ability to dust that chandelier, particularly while pregnant. In my house-icon of the Annunciation, Mary turns to the angel with household spinning still in hand. There's something in the sacred plainness of her ordinary tasks arrested that I can believe in, and trust that here at least, beauty will carry one safely to the Good.

Mary Townsend, Queens, NY
Townsend is an assistant professor of philosophy at St. John's University in Queens, New York.

Utagawa Kuniyoshi, Landscape and Beauties – Feeling Like Reading the Next Volume

Is Community Possible without Faith?

On Eberhard Arnold's "Why We Live in Community: A Manifesto," Autumn 2018: The call of the gospel necessarily impels us toward a different mode of living; this mode must be oriented toward the community of God's people. This is the heart of Arnold's manifesto, and to it I assent completely.

Yet I worry that Arnold understates the power of common grace. It's a criticism that has been leveled at my own tradition: Calvinists are sometimes accused of believing that man is utterly depraved rather than totally

Vincent van Gogh, *Old Man Reading*

depraved. The distinction is significant: The former says that we are completely given over to evil; the latter that there is no part of us untouched by sin. When we embrace the latter doctrine, we can add that because of God's common grace – he freely gives good gifts to all people everywhere – we can recognize in nearly any human community some traces of leftover goodness not totally erased by the Fall.

Evangelical theologian Scot McKnight refers to this vestige as a cracked icon – something beautiful that, though marred, can still reveal true traces of its former grandeur. The Reformed missionary Francis Schaeffer spoke of "glorious ruins."

I wonder if Arnold does not overstate the degree of damage to these icons and erosion to the ruins. He writes, "Here it becomes abundantly clear that the realization of true community, the actual building up of a communal life, is impossible without faith in a higher Power."

Surely this exaggerates the degree to which the natural order has fallen. Certainly, faith in God is necessary to realize what my church's confession calls "the chief end of man:" to glorify God and enjoy him forever. But even in an unregenerate state, human beings can and regularly do form communities that reflect some truth about the world and about humanity, and do so in a significant enough way that I am loathe to call them "false" communities, which seems to be implied by Arnold's manifesto.

We have all known happy marriages that, even without knowledge of God, show forth the beauty of married life. We have seen neighborhoods and small towns filled with people who do not know Jesus and yet model genuine care and love for one another. These communities might be incomplete, but to call them "false" seems to minimize the traces of common grace still displayed in their members.

What this manifesto can do, however, is to remind us that these communities are incomplete: that each is called to be transformed by the Holy Spirit through the faith of the community members, and thus to become completely itself, and a part of the complete community that is the kingdom of God.

Jake Meador, Lincoln, NE

Reading Icons

On Navid Kermani's "It Could Be Anyone," Autumn 2018: Kermani's description of Caravaggio's *The Calling of Saint Matthew* is perceptive and impressive, rooted in the painting's form itself. In particular, I admire his analysis of how the figures interact along with other elements to create this feeling of both immediacy and confusion – an effect that Caravaggio evokes in many of his paintings. Kermani seems to have a natural understanding of how Caravaggio seamlessly integrates these formal qualities with the actual content of the work: the strange, abrupt, and confusing story of Saint Matthew's call.

It's this same careful attention to the aesthetics of the work itself that I wish he had brought to the first piece he considers: the early icon of Mary in the convent of Santa Maria del Rosario. Icon painters are known as *icon writers,* and as Kermani read Caravaggio's painting, so I would love to hear his reading of the image of Mary.

Edmond Rochat, New York, NY

Plough Mailbag

What a breath of fresh air *Plough* brings to me! When the magazine arrives, I prepare a cup of tea, then carefully remove the outer protective packaging and just hold the magazine: sensing the contents, feeling its weight and the texture of the cover. Then I peruse the contents, looking at the artwork and reading the poetry. At the next sitting I delve into the essays, reading one or two depending on my schedule. By then several days have passed and I sigh, finishing my ritual – letting the issue sit on my desk for a while longer before placing the magazine among other issues of *Plough Quarterly* that I've purchased over the years. The articles and artwork stay with me for weeks. *Plough* has become an essential part of my spiritual and personal growth.

Diane Turner-Forte, Ellerbe, NC

We welcome letters to the editor. Letters and web comments may be edited for length and clarity, and may be published in any medium. Letters should be sent with the writer's name and address to letters@plough.com. ➤

INTRODUCING

Plough Spiritual Guides

Backpack Classics for Modern Pilgrims

plough.com/guides

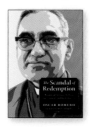

Love in the Void

Where God Finds Us

Simone Weil
Edited by Laurie Gagne

The Scandal of Redemption

When God Liberates the Poor, Saves Sinners, and Heals Nations

Oscar Romero
Foreword by Michael Lapsley

The Reckless Way of Love

Notes on Following Jesus

Dorothy Day
Introduction by D. L. Mayfield

The Two Ways

The Early Christian Vision of Discipleship from The Didache *and* The Shepherd of Hermas

Introduction by Rowan Williams

Now is Eternity

Comfort and Wisdom for Difficult Hours

J. C. Blumhardt
and C. F. Blumhardt

The son of one of the twenty-one Coptic Christians killed by ISIS in 2015 touches the face of his father, Hany. The icons of the martyrs are in a church in El-Aour, Egypt.

The Twenty-One Coptic Christians

In a carefully choreographed propaganda video released in February 2015, ISIS militants behead twenty-one orange-clad Christian men on a Libyan beach. As the video records, in their final moments the men were praying to Jesus – just like the early Christians did centuries ago when dying at the hands of Roman persecutors. It's the recency of their voluntary death that unsettles the modern mind. What's

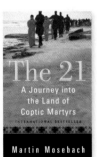

well accepted as an edifying act of heroism in an ancient saint is shocking when it surfaces in a YouTube video.

Since 2015, the threat of ISIS has receded, and new headline atrocities have supplanted this grisly event in the public consciousness, at least in America and Europe. But not in the Egyptian homeland of Coptic Christianity from which all but one of the murdered came. While they lived, they were migrant workers from impoverished villages, just like millions of others around the

world, with nothing to mark them out as special; several were fathers with wives and young children at home. Yet today the twenty-one are venerated by the Coptic Orthodox Church as saints, and miracles are ascribed to their intercession.

What makes a modern martyr? To find out, the German literary novelist Martin Mosebach traveled to the Egyptian village of El-Aour to meet their families and better understand the faith and culture that shaped such conviction. His book, *The 21: A Journey into the Land of Coptic Martyrs,* which was a bestseller in Germany when it appeared in spring 2018, will be published in English by *Plough* in February 2019.

In his book, the author described how he began his project:

There are so many historic martyrs we know so little about, other than a few inaccurate details about their death; the dry lists of the *Martyrologium Romanum,* the Catholic Church's official register of saints, remained abstract until Christian art turned them into tangible, relatable images. Things are rather different with the Twenty-One: not only is there a video of their Passion, but this video has the selfsame intention and effect as a work of art, albeit a particularly vile one – it is at once both document and aesthetically staged, pathetic concoction. . . .

The Twenty-One could well have echoed the words of Paul the Apostle: "for we are made a spectacle unto the world, and to angels, and to men." But before they became such a spectacle for God and the world, each led the unremarkable life of a poor farmer. So was there anything in their villages that might have foreshadowed all this? In February and March of 2017, two years after the massacre, I traveled to Upper Egypt, to the homes they had left when they set out for Libya in search of work.

To mark the fourth anniversary of the martyrdom, Mosebach and Coptic Archbishop Angaelos of London will be speaking in three cities in February 2019: in New York on February 11, at an evening with *New Yorker* journalist Eliza Griswold; in Washington, DC, on February 12, at a conference at the National Press Club with the Religious Freedom Institute; and in London on February 14, at an ecumenical commemoration at Westminster. *Plough* readers interested in attending these events can get in touch at *info@plough.com.*

Nehemiah House

Comfortably settled in suburbia, Patrick Murray had a thriving law practice when friends asked him and his wife, Debbie, to help pray for someone to join their inner-city youth ministry. After several months of persistent prayer, Debbie told him she believed *they* were the couple God was calling. He wasn't eager to exchange their secure life for an uncertain future. But they were, after all, Christians. Selling their home in Westfield, Massachusetts, in 2002 the Murrays took up residence in the low-income, high-crime Six Corners neighborhood of Springfield. Inspired by the story of Nehemiah rebuilding Jerusalem's walls, they called their community Nehemiah House. You might find them and others who have joined them praying across the street from drug

dealers and prostitutes, transforming a trash-strewn lot into a garden, or gathered for a meal with asylum seekers. Their goal, they say, is to piece together the fragmented lives of those they encounter with Christ's love.

Poet in This Issue: Christian Wiman

 Born in Snyder, Texas, in 1966, and raised as a Southern Baptist, Christian Wiman once described the environment of his upbringing as having been "saturated with religion." However, during his years in college and for decades after, the religion of his childhood faded to near nonexistence. Wiman studied at Washington and Lee University, and while spending a semester studying at Oxford became interested in the poetry of William Butler Yeats and T. S. Eliot, which inspired him to begin writing poetry of his own. He spent time teaching at Stanford University, Northwestern University, and Lynchburg College, then served as editor of *Poetry* magazine from 2003 to 2013. On his thirty-ninth birthday, less than eight months after his wedding, Wiman was diagnosed with a rare and incurable cancer. This led to a renewal of faith of sorts, about which Wiman said, "I was just finally able to assent to the faith that had long been latent within me." This is reflected in his recent work, including the poems on pages 35 and 36. Wiman is the author of eleven books of poetry, prose, and poems in translation. He currently teaches at Yale Divinity School and the Institute of Sacred Music, and lives in New Haven, Connecticut, with his wife and twin daughters. ➤

Verena Arnold

MAUREEN SWINGER

"I ONLY HAD AN eighth-grade education," she loved to remind us editors whenever she'd spotted a howler. Verena Arnold, a long-time proofreader for *Plough,* usually got the printout of a book just before it went to press. By that stage, the text had already been scrutinized for errors. Verena's check came near the end – "the disaster check," in house jargon. With unnerving regularity, she caught disasters others had failed to see: the missing word, the garbled sentence, nonsensical punctuation.

Verena's schooling may have stopped at eighth grade, but she was a voracious reader. Having grown up in the Paraguayan outback – she was one of twelve children born to Swiss pacifist émigrés – English wasn't her mother tongue. (She immigrated to the United States in 1961 at age twenty-two.) Yet decades of reading had given her a sense for the language that outmatched that of many English majors.

She came to publishing in later life, after raising her own eight children and serving for decades with her husband, Johann Christoph Arnold, a pastor and author who for eighteen years was elder of the Bruderhof. She started by helping to proofread the twelve books he published with *Plough* beginning in the mid-1990s. In recent years, she branched out, with numerous *Plough* titles eventually going through her hands.

It was often a mystery where she found the time. Born in 1938, she was in her seventies now. Yet she and Johann Christoph still took an active role in the international Bruderhof movement; after fifty years of marriage, they were virtually inseparable. With him, Verena met with popes and presidents. She also visited prison inmates on death row.

Then, eighteen months ago, she became a widow. She continued to carry on the pastoral task that she and her husband had shared, usually meeting daily with several individuals or couples. Even so, this venerable grandmother of forty-four and great-grandmother of six still showed up daily in the community laundry, where she folded T-shirts and sorted jeans for the three hundred fellow members.

Verena Arnold,
1938–2018

Verena got much of her proof-reading done out in nature: she would take a stack of papers and her camera – she was a wildlife photographer – and head to a favorite spot in the nearby woods. In white-tail season, that spot would be a hunting blind and she'd bring a rifle. She'd mark commas while waiting for a deer to come into range.

Verena's legendary forthrightness could make you squirm, but came laced with humor and a disarming humility. Intensely competitive, especially when it came to a card game, she had a rebellious streak, too, and enjoyed confounding expectations. Nothing was more certain to draw her rebuke than praise. Probably she disapproves of this article.

If so, she is disapproving in heaven. Verena died on September 21 after a five-year battle with cancer. She will be missed immeasurably – as Cardinal Dolan of New York announced at her wake, "A matriarch has gone home." And if you, *Plough* reader, start noticing more typos, this is why: in her new home she's been given greater tasks to do. ⌦

Maureen Swinger is an editor at Plough.

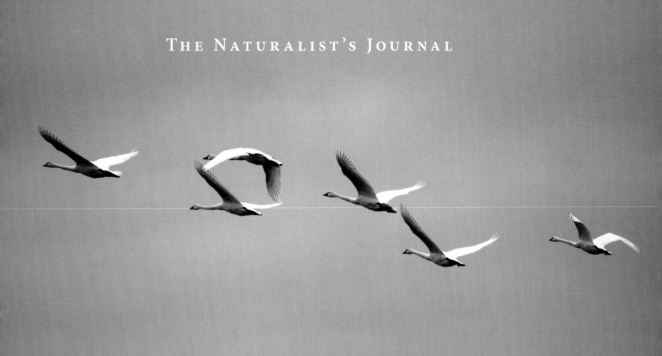

Tundra Swans

DWIGHT WAREHAM

I HAD JUST CLIMBED out of bed when I heard it: the unmistakable calling of tundra swans. It was still dark, so I rushed to the window, opened it wide, and put my face up to the screen to listen. The bugling chorus of what may have been more than one hundred swans passed close, then moved off toward the horizon.

Just fifteen minutes later I was stepping out of the house when I heard the wild calling of a second flock. It sounded like they were directly overhead. Looking up, I could see stars shining between the cumulus clouds. Suddenly the swans appeared in this clear patch of sky in a beautiful wide-angled V – somewhere between one hundred and one hundred and fifty swans. They appeared snow white against the black sky, illuminated by the lights of a nearby resort. The birds vanished to the northeast, honking continually their mysterious-sounding call. While I was watching this, a shooting star streaked across the early dawn sky.

The third flock showed up just as the pupils began to arrive at the school where I was teaching. By now it was broad daylight, and the children and I watched the thirty-two swans together – our first lesson of the day, and a grand one.

Dwight Wareham is an avid naturalist and a veteran elementary school teacher. He lives at Maple Ridge, a Bruderhof in Esopus, New York.

JOHN THORNTON

Universities can shape their students for life – in ways they don't intend.

A Debt to

Education

65 ·
45 · −
48 · −
38 · +
10 · −
56 · −
45 · +
82 · −
80 · −
52 · +
18 · +
90 · +
89 · −
98 · −
88 · −
09 · +
34 · −
68 · +
55 · +
98 · −
65 · +
45 · −
48 · −
38 · +
10 · −
56 · −
51 · +
82 · −
80 · −
587 · −
248 · −

As universities never tire of pointing out, education is more than the mere transmission of knowledge. It is about formation. Professors and administrators all impressed this upon me often during my years as an undergraduate and later at seminary. At Baylor, a Baptist institution, this took the form of weekly chapel services and university-sponsored mission trips. At Duke Divinity School, students gathered regularly in "spiritual formation groups." Formation at both institutions meant not just studying but developing habits, disciplining desires, and living in a community of supportive people in order to foster a particular character.

It worked. My university studies made me who I am by shaping how I approach not only my pastoral work but also politics, economics, race, gender, sexuality, and society.

Yet my university experiences also formed me in other, less obvious ways. They made me into a person whose life choices – from which job to take, to how many children to have – are in large part determined by my student debts.

We don't often talk of the formative nature of debt in the same way we do in regard to other educational experiences. But just as education is about more than funneling information into students' brains, indebtedness is about more than the transfer of money. Universities rarely address the aspect of higher education that may most powerfully shape students' futures: the debt they take on to finance it.

A few hours spent watching promotional videos for universities, whether public or private, illustrates the point. These commercials display a remarkable consistency. Wide shots of buildings chosen to match what prospective students presumably imagine a campus to look like; a montage of student athletes competing; an articulate voiceover offering an inspiring narration about students finding themselves. There's always an image of teenagers studying in a library. In these commercials, almost without exception, universities tout the difference that their graduates make in the world. They rarely mention future earnings.

Visually, they relay this message of empowerment by including as many scenes outside the classroom as inside. They convince students that university education serves not just to help them get a leg up in the market, but to shape them into particular kinds of people for the

John Thornton is a Baptist pastor in Winston-Salem, North Carolina.

sake of a common future. In the words of the University of Alabama website, this goal is an education that "produces socially-conscious, ethical and well-rounded leaders who are grounded in their subject matter and capable of controlling their own destinies."

It's a grand vision that echoes a tradition stretching back to Plato. However, those espousing it rarely seem to reckon with the possibility that students' debts might prohibit them from ever being "capable of controlling their own destinies."

Debt forms us just as radically as a university curriculum does. As bills mount, debt becomes a guiding force in our lives, directing our decisions about where to live, where to work, how to save and spend, and what we imagine possible. The anxiety, regret, and shame over one's inability to determine one's own life shapes our souls as well. In a deeply

moving essay in *The Baffler,* M. H. Miller describes his working-class family's struggles with the $120,000 in debt they assumed to enable him to attend New York University: "The delicate balancing act my family and I perform in order to make a payment each month has become the organizing principle of our lives." If student debt forms us in this way, we'd do well to ask what kind of formation it is.

Student debt occupies a prominent place in the US economy. In 2018, Americans carried $1.5 trillion in student loan debt. The average 2016 graduate had $37,000 in loans. Forty-four million Americans have student loans, meaning roughly one quarter of the population is shaped and formed by the monthly payment they must make.

All debt forms us, but it's important to recognize how student debt shapes our conception of ourselves and our society in a way

Above: Margaret McWethy, What's on the Table?

Previous spread: Margaret McWethy, Jif

different than other ways one can owe money. Credit card debt or payday loans, for example, often result from emergencies. Car loans are a rent for needed transportation. We can leverage mortgage debt for wealth building. For all our grand visions of education and formation, when it comes to finances we usually talk about how student loans enable a borrower to attain a professional qualification that moves them into a higher income bracket. In a capitalist society in which every choice requires a financial calculation, looking at student debt as a matter of calculated choices forms us in distinct ways that warrant our attention.

The Retributive View

One way of framing indebtedness as an individual choice is retributive. It looks backward to the past: students could have made different choices to avoid or mitigate their debt. They could have chosen majors that pay more or schools with higher rates of success in the market. They could have worked a second or third job. They could have eaten ramen at home instead of going out.

Because of all this, people with the retributive view don't believe debtors worthy of grace. Adopting the retributive view conveniently gets them off the hook for any obligation they might have toward those in debt. The debtors could have chosen otherwise.

Take my own case. I didn't have to go to Duke Divinity School. I could have chosen a more affordable seminary (plenty of pastors complete an online degree); I could have worked harder and gotten better grades, and so earned more scholarships; I could have put more hours into part-time jobs. To the last point, one semester during my studies I worked two late night shifts a week at a coffee shop on campus in addition to the twenty hours I worked tutoring middle school students.

After a few weeks I decided that the extra $75 I earned wasn't worth the exhaustion I felt in class the next day. Of course, I could've chosen to stick with it and knocked a few hundred dollars off the $47,000 debt I graduated with.

I recognize my own privilege in this scenario. Millions of people deal with far more challenging circumstances, far deeper holes to climb out of. Almost all of my classmates did. I'm a relatively healthy single white male. These institutions were made by and for people like me. But they were also made to divide all of us in the name of consumer choice.

There's a particular blindness involved in looking at student debt as a consumer choice. I remember one graduate school administrator expressing judgment that students complained about debt when so many of them paid for cable television. That year the average student graduated with $44,000 in loans. I struggle to imagine how choosing to forgo ESPN and HGTV would have made a significant difference, but that wasn't the point. The point was the assignment of blame on students for failing to calculate the cost of their choices.

Bean counting aside, if we question the choice of going to a particular school or studying a particular subject, we also question the goods that came from those choices. Can we still love someone and say he should have gone to a different school from the one where he met his spouse? What about the person who discovered her calling to ministry at a particular school? Of course some people should have chosen otherwise, but when we reduce the basis of those choices to the strictly economic, we reduce people's entire lives to a string of consumer choices. In doing so we accept an alienation – from ourselves and from each other – because education, like other goods, *isn't* just one more consumer choice.

BUSINESS REPLY MAIL

FIRST-CLASS MAIL   PERMIT NO. 332   CONGERS, NY

POSTAGE WILL BE PAID BY ADDRESSEE

PLOUGH QUARTERLY
PO BOX 345
CONGERS NY 10920-9895

Margaret McWethy, *Chicken Noodle*

The Redemptive View

This retributive view with its emphasis on regret often clears the way for another way of framing consumer choice, one that promises redemptive hope.

A few months ago the Cooperative Baptist Fellowship awarded grants of $10,000 each to me and about a dozen other ministers so we could pay off debt. Having determined that debt plays an important, damaging role in the lives of ministers, CBF's Ministerial Excellence Initiative combines immediate financial relief with two gatherings to discuss finances and ministry, and a year of financial advising. The first session was a kind of crash course in basic financial literacy, similar to that taught by Dave Ramsey. Over the two days of the training, we consistently heard two messages. First, we ought not to lose sleep over finding ourselves in debt. We shouldn't feel guilty about the underwater mortgage, the unexpected pregnancy, the student debt for seminary. All of the ministers spoke with refreshing candor about how their financial struggles affected their ministerial work. All of us admitted to living with a loneliness brought on by believing that we couldn't publicly discuss our personal finances for fear of appearing ungrateful. I've heard my fair share of retributive cruelty about my indebtedness, so I found the words of grace spoken by the instructors and ministers remarkably refreshing.

However, I noticed that choice and guilt came back in when we talked about the future. The second message we heard repeatedly was that though significant unavoidable decisions in the past got us into debt, a myriad of small ones in the future could accumulate to get us out. Like most financial literacy trainers, the instructors pinpointed discreet purchases as the way to save money and get out of debt. They never said it quite so plainly, but I heard that we *ought to* feel guilty when choosing wants over needs in our future consumer spending. Repeatedly the trainer used the example of eating peanut butter at home versus Mexican food at a restaurant. So while I shouldn't feel bad about choosing Duke over a more affordable seminary, I deserve the consequences of choosing La Hacienda over Jif. In a conversation we spoke at length about how we all needed to purchase cheaper toilet paper. No one brought up the possibility of increased medical bills brought on by eating exclusively peanut butter, but it seemed to me like something we ought to consider when calculating expected future expenses.

At one point I mentioned what seemed to be a rather obvious incongruity between the two messages. I made reference to the 2004 paper by Elizabeth Warren called "The

Over-Consumption Myth," in which she writes that American families spend roughly the same amount as previous generations on consumer goods. Spending on consumer goods has not driven people into debt. Rather, the rising costs of fixed goods like housing, healthcare, and education, combined with stagnant wages, have. In our training session, these statistics were dismissed: they troubled the narrative of redemptive choice.

Financial literacy is a kind of formation of its own. Such programs form us to believe that we can make up for one $40,000 decision with forty thousand *other* decisions that save a single dollar each. In retrospect, it seems fitting that Duke Divinity School required each of us to sit through a brief seminar on financial literacy prior to graduation. The school needed one last moment to shape us as individuals in control of our destiny through wise choices, hard work, and willpower.

Demonization

Ultimately this formation of graduates as debtors-by-choice serves an important function within our political economy. It changes the problem of debt and higher education from one of collective, political responsibility to one of individual consumer decisions. And it completely ignores what role the broader political economic system plays in our indebtedness.

In his book *Neoliberalism's Demons,* Adam Kotsko writes that the emphasis on individual responsibility in free-market capitalism bears a striking resemblance to the traditional Christian story of the origin of the devil and of demons. In order to explain evil in the world, this story – which, though ancient, is not found in the Bible – has been used to get God off the hook, so to speak, by blaming the devil. The logic runs like this: Why does evil exist? Because God made creatures with freedom of choice, and they've chosen to act sinfully. That God knew they would sin provides no reason to hold God responsible. God's goodness remains intact while evil continues.

Whatever the merits of this theodicy, it's not hard to see how it parallels the way we give God-like status to capitalism in today's economic cosmos. While we may acknowledge that market forces might influence a decision, we still hold consumers responsible for their individual choices and demand that they must bear the consequences. Capitalism can't bear responsibility for the bad outcomes that happen in its system, just as, according to Christian belief, God retains God's goodness in the face of evil.

This economic theology of capitalism makes *us* the demons in the story, the ones to blame when things go wrong. Think, for instance, of the common idea that individual recycling can stave off climate change – this in spite of the fact that one hundred companies produce 71 percent of carbon emissions. The political economic system and its most powerful actors remain in place while we scramble about arguing over one another's plastic drinking straws.

Student debt is thus just one way in which the theology of capitalism "demonizes" people, especially the poor and those who belong to vulnerable minorities, by making them solely responsible for their misfortunes. It justifies the status quo by distracting from the political and economic forces beyond any one person's control. Applied to the question of student debt, the logic of demonization says that while

> We need a theology that says we belong to one another.

a college degree could lead to the benefits of increased income, it will very often bring too high a debt load. If it does, students should consider giving up the expensive degree and the debt it brings. If they do not, they rightly are to blame.

But that conclusion ignores a larger reality. A recently released paper by Julie Margetta Morgan and Marshall Steinbaum argues that "credentialization" – the need for higher degrees to get a better job – has driven up the cost of higher education and student debt. They discovered that while it's true that those with a college degree still earn more than those without, this is because wages for those without degrees have gone down. Put another way, a higher degree provides a benefit but it does so because the potential risk of *not* attaining one has greatly increased. Going to college is no longer about moving up the ladder, but the only way to avoid falling down. The study's authors find that this holds especially true for minorities.

Universities, facing their own financial crunch as public funding decreases, have added new degree programs eligible for available loan dollars. They know that students in need of yet another degree to remain competitive will enroll, making student loan dollars available to make up for decreased public funding. Morgan and Steinbaum write, "Colleges thus increase their revenue, since they know that demand will be forthcoming from students with no other option if they want to get a job."

Student debt thus exposes a farther-reaching cruelty in a system that treats people, in the end, as autonomous consumers. Until we recognize the deeper problem, we will be hindered from taking collective action to build better lives together. We spend so much time blaming one another and ourselves that we don't have time to look at bigger, collective

solutions like tuition-free higher education or the cancellation of student loan debt. We don't ask what kind of society we want to see and what kind of collective political action it might take to win it. Our eyes haven't been trained to see society and its institutions as something we can change. Our imaginations haven't been formed to desire something better fitted for human flourishing.

Cathleen Rehfield, *Stacked Cups*

Counter-Formation

If economic failure is essentially a personal matter, then so is success. Flourishing would then be an individualistic, zero-sum game, not something gained and enjoyed together. That this lie seems plausible to so many is a symptom of the extent to which neoliberal habits have de-formed us.

To remedy this, we need a kind of counter-formation. Any alternative, any resistance offered by Christians or others will require a community dedicated to the collective sharing of resources with the aim of achieving a world without interminable debt. For all its complicity in capitalism's inhumanities, I can't help but think that one such community should be the church: a community that lives in a way that accords better with the kingdom proclaimed by Jesus.

This counter-formation to combat the effects of capitalism would have to look a lot like what we see in university formation. It would have to reform desire, shape concrete action, and guide decision-making about how we use collective resources. Instead of treating people as isolated consumers, each individually responsible for her own fate, we need a theology that says we belong to one another. We must bear one another's burdens, including our debts. We need a theology that preaches a freedom that's more substantial than the freedom to earn and spend.

During the middle of our sessions on financial literacy, we took a break from discussing toilet paper and peanut butter and gathered in a circle. One by one, a member of each pastor's congregation looked that pastor in the eye and described what he or she meant to their church. They told their pastors of their excitement for them to experience the financial freedom that the grant moved them toward. And one by one, they gave each a check for $10,000. We all shed a few tears, knowing the difference such an amount made. And in that moment each of us saw that we could do better. We could treat one another as human beings ought to – neither as reckless spenders deserving of retributive penalties, nor as "financially literate" spenders committed to years of penny-pinching.

I think back to that moment, the one all of us would say powerfully moved us. I imagine what a community might look like that believed Jesus' prayer for the forgiveness of debts "on earth as in heaven." I think to myself what such a community of believers might do with its money, how they might use it to pay for the debts of others. I don't see such a community here, but I can imagine it – and the mere ability to imagine this alternative world gives some measure of hope.

Another world *is* possible, a world without interminable debt. We can create a world together in which we are formed to see each other not as lonely individual consumers but as comrades creating a world of collectively shared goods. A different world lies waiting somewhere in the undetermined future, but we can't build it individually. If we want to see it in our lifetimes, we'll have to make it together. ⤳

Another world *is* possible, a world without interminable debt.

What's the Good of a School?

Helping your child flourish means not putting her first.

D. L. MAYFIELD

I KNOW EVERY PARENT says this, but it's true: my daughter is brilliant. She taught herself to read when she was four. She has always been sensitive, prone to anxiety, her mind always a few steps ahead of every story. When she tested into the gifted and talented program at her school, we weren't all that surprised.

I was primarily homeschooled, so I was intrigued by the entire process. It raised questions about my values for education – not just for my daughter, but for our country as a whole. According to federal guidelines, all public schools must provide resources to identify and support "gifted" students. The general assumption is that gifted students are bright, deserving of harder classes and more engagement. But this isn't always the case. As my daughter's second grade teacher told us, there are differences between "bright" and "gifted"

D. L. Mayfield works with refugee communities and is the author of Assimilate or Go Home: Notes from a Failed Missionary on Rediscovering Faith *(HarperOne, 2016). She lives in Portland, Oregon, with her husband and two children.*

learners – the former tend to be high-achieving performers, while the latter can often struggle in academics.

Giftedness, as some educators are learning to describe it, really is an issue of asynchronous development: a child's brain might be able to understand and absorb complex math problems, while socially he fails to pick up nonverbal cues and is left out of games. There is also rising awareness of advanced learning capabilities occurring simultaneously with other conditions such as attention deficit hyperactivity disorder, obsessive compulsive disorder, or others – these students are called twice exceptional (2e) learners.

What, exactly, did I want my gifted child to get out of her education?

Here in the United States, where education is seen both as a right and a competition, I find the tension between loving our neighbors and advocating for our own children is exemplified by gifted programs. I started to ask questions: Who gets identified as gifted? Which schools end up getting those coveted extra resources? And what, exactly, did I want my gifted child to get out of her education?

That last question is probably one we should be asking ourselves more. I would say that a good school leaves students feeling safe and cared for, serves all of its students equally, and imparts to its students curiosity about the world – the key to a lifetime of learning. For others, the answer might include challenging academics, a push to become better citizens, or preparation for successful jobs.

AND YET, this is not how schools are often measured or discussed. At least in my circle of acquaintance, people often learn about their local public schools from websites that rank them according to standardized test scores. Do such ratings reflect social and emotional intelligence, student involvement, community impact, or a culture of care? They do not; nor do these ratings rely on the witness of teachers, students, and parents – arguably the best experts on how the school is doing.

As educators have proposed, coming up with metrics that better reflect our actual values (including things like teaching environment, civic engagement, resource allocation, and academic progress) could help us identify schools that are truly working for every child in the community.

When Jack Schneider, author of *Beyond Test Scores,* became frustrated with how his own neighborhood school was rated, he set about researching why this happened. Schneider points out that when we began to view education as a private good instead of a public good, it became a race for the best education. In economics this is called a positional good – your education is only worth something if it's somehow better than another person's. Because of this, there is little incentive to put resources into lower-achieving schools, and segregation and inequality persist and thrive.

Schneider then explores measures of success that can't always be tested. Together with other researchers, educators, and scholars, he is working to change how schools in his state of Massachusetts are analyzed – including how staff, students, and community members view their school as an important part of assessment. In a sense, Schneider and others are advocating that these actual stakeholders know best how a school is serving the community. This type of analysis takes more work, but I believe it is the right step toward ensuring that all schools are places of flourishing for all children.

By classifying schools as good or bad,

failing or desirable, entire neighborhoods have been changed. People with means move into neighborhoods with "good" schools, driving up prices that ensure lower-income families won't be able to afford to live there. In an unequal system, choice leads to concentrations of lower-income communities that are often left with fewer resources for their schools.

Isn't the goal that every child should flourish? It seems to be the goal behind the US Department of Education's mission, "to promote student achievement . . . by fostering educational excellence and ensuring equal access." But as I have found in my own state of Oregon, this isn't reality. While discrimination based on race or income is against the law, upwardly mobile parents have found ways to rig the system in their favor, often under the guise of doing what is best for their own children. In a Christian culture that often encourages people to focus on their families, this practice has been baptized in the name of common sense. Meanwhile, the common good in our own communities has suffered. Public schools

in the United States continue to be segregated both by income and race, which results in resources not being equitably allocated to our country's children.

Programs for giftedness in public schools are one example of this bigger issue. Our local elementary school on the outskirts of Portland has a student population that is 56 percent Hispanic and 20 percent white. Ninety-four percent of students qualify for the free and reduced lunch program, which means they live close to or below the poverty line. It is also incredibly rich in culture, with over twenty-seven languages spoken inside its walls.

Our school of just under five hundred students has eight kids that tested into the gifted program – less than 2 percent of the population. Half of those students are white. Overall, the rates of students being identified as gifted are low and, while the program director tells me that they are actively working for more equity in those numbers, they don't yet match the school's racial makeup. The reason seems to be that neither teachers nor standardized testing do well at identifying the wide variety of gifted learners, especially those from

different cultural or ethnic backgrounds.

By contrast, one of the "best" school districts in the state has vastly different numbers. One highly rated elementary school is 88 percent white, has less than 8 percent of students on free and reduced lunch, and fully 5 percent of the student body tested into the gifted program. Are the students at this school inherently smarter because more are white and fewer are poor? Or is something else going on here?

These kinds of disparities affect students around the country. In a *New York Times* article on the gifted program in Charlottesville, Virginia, journalists argue that these programs have been used to re-segregate the school system in many parts of the country. According to federal data, in 1984 only 11 percent of Charlottesville's white students qualified as gifted. By 2003, about a third of white students qualified – and currently white students in Charlottesville are six times as likely to be in advanced courses as black students.

This is just one picture of how race affects the public education system. Since the 1954 *Brown v. Board of Education* ruling there have been many ways that white parents have

avoided truly integrating schools. Sadly, many Christians have been involved in this, with private Christian schools and homeschooling movements directly contributing to a new kind of segregation – one based not on overtly racist rhetoric, but predicated on the idea of the right to personal choice.

School choice has also been a vehicle of equality, however. As Nicole Baker Fulgham points out in *Educating All God's Children,* African American pastors, along with increasing numbers of Latino and Hispanic clergy, have pushed for alternatives for children in habitually under-performing communities – either by starting their own schools or by requesting vouchers for charter and private schools. Baker observes that while she recognizes the way Christians in non-white majority neighborhoods have often fought for justice in the school system, she has yet to see a large-scale, coordinated push for educational justice that would help all children.

Overall, it might be time to pay attention to the impact of prioritizing school choice, which overwhelmingly benefits the privileged. The free-market approach to education has led to higher concentrations of low-income children in local schools. It is re-segregating the system.

WHAT IS THE RIGHT relationship to educational choice for the Christian? It's complicated, and I often think about what Paul was trying to communicate in Galatians: it is for freedom that Christ has set us free. "For you were called to freedom, brothers. Only do not use your freedom as an opportunity for the flesh, but through love serve one another. For the whole law is fulfilled in one word: 'you shall love your neighbor as yourself'" (5:1, 13–14). Paul, a shrewd observer of humanity, anticipated that the allure of freedom can sometimes result in our selfish natures seeking the best for ourselves, meanwhile forgetting our responsibility to our neighbors.

How do we love and educate our precious, unique, smart children in a world driven by outward measures of success and a fear of scarcity of resources? This continues to be a question for my family. I am still surprised by how easy it is to slip into the mindset of wanting what is best for my child, perhaps even at the expense of others.

Although my daughter was identified as gifted last year, there is not a lot that her school offers in the way of enrichment for such kids. Last year it depended upon the goodness of a teacher willing to forgo lunch once a week to provide programming. This year, there have been no meetings, no extra work, and only a vague action plan to encourage my daughter to read a wider variety of books. As her parent, I feel torn, driven by a desire to see her capabilities challenged. But I have slowly been interrogating my motives and my fears. In the underpaid and understaffed world of Title I schools, advocating for extra resources for less than 2 percent of the population strikes me as

immoral – or at least, part of the problem.

Instead, working together with other parents and teachers, we continue to build resources that will benefit a wider range of students: bringing back the Scholastic book fair, starting a team of kids to compete in a local reading program, pushing to have a mural painted outside the school to celebrate the joyful diversity inside its walls. Recently a parent leadership group has formed, and parents from a wide variety of backgrounds are raising their voices and ask for improvements – including an increase in academic work that challenges their children. Together we are making the school continue to work for everyone – as racial and socio-economic integration has been consistently shown to do.

It's hard to overestimate how strongly the desire for success shapes our society. But the end result is the same: resources are consolidated, snatched up, and segregated. Now more than ever, schools with high rates of poverty are abandoned in favor of better test scores. And all of us have a part to play in this. As people of faith, do we want to pursue the "best" for our children? Or when Paul says, "knowledge puffs up, but true love builds up," do we take him at his word?

> I easily slip into the mindset of wanting what is best for my child – even at the expense of others.

MY DAUGHTER LOVES her school. Her character – who she is at her core – is being built up not just by her classmates (many of them refugees and immigrants from places we see constantly in the news headlines) but by teachers, staff, parents, and community members. She, unlike

me, is growing up with an awareness of how to navigate real differences in religion, culture, race, and academics, and she is being given the gift of being in the minority (which could come in handy in the future, as the United States continues to grow more diverse).

And our local school, which from some perspectives looks like it is lacking in resources or pathways for gifted students, does something even more valuable: it is a sanctuary, one of the few spaces in our city and community that is committed to helping everyone, no matter their situation. Entering its doors, I sometimes almost feel like it is a sacred space; it is one of the few places where I have seen any child welcomed – no matter her ethnic and socio-economic identity, her cognitive or physical ability. This is a place that mirrors what Jesus tells us of the kingdom of God, where the people our society ignores are treated as valuable, and as blessed.

I think of my daughter, and even myself, in light of words like "giftedness" or "talent" and how they orient me in the direction of individualism and fear, in the direction of always having the best. This is the pursuit of the kind of knowledge that Paul says "puffs up" – distancing us from our neighbors and leading to harm and inequality. This is why I agree with the experts that giftedness is better understood as asynchronous development – when parts of our mind, or perhaps even our socio-emotional intelligence, advance faster than other parts. All of us have areas where we need to grow, where we need to be built up. All of us are hindered in our quest to better love God by loving our neighbors – perhaps by fear, or selfishness, or an idolization of success.

In the end, I don't want what is best for my daughter according to our society. I want what is best for all of God's kids, which is why I continue to long for the day when we orient ourselves accordingly, and choose to put resources into the places that have deliberately been ignored. Real education builds up – and it always starts at the very bottom, because that is where we learn how to love and be loved by our neighbors. ➘

A School of One

MICHAEL ST. THOMAS

A review of *Rethinking School: How to Take Charge of Your Child's Education*
Susan Wise Bauer (W. W. Norton), 288 pages

TO BEGIN WITH, the American public school system was a response to immigration. Faced with the challenge of assimilating the "huddled masses" that had arrived on American shores, during the 1840s US Secretary of Education Horace Mann implemented a model invented by the Prussians: age-graded classrooms. Many similar models spread through Europe in the wake of the Industrial Revolution with the goal of educating the urban poor and shaping national identity. Critics, however, compared these efficient and replicable new systems to factories in which children were treated impersonally. Charles Dickens famously satirized British schools in his 1854 novel *Hard Times*, in which the inauspiciously named Mr. Gradgrind presides over hundreds of "little pitchers" who sit in rows, waiting to be filled with "imperial gallons of facts."

Michael St. Thomas is the head of the Humanities program at the Portsmouth Abbey School in Rhode Island.

> When children discover
> something they love,
> they pursue it with an
> eagerness that never seems
> to exhaust them.

One and a half centuries later, Susan Wise Bauer follows suit in her book *Rethinking School: How to Take Charge of Your Child's Education*. Though American schools today look different than they did in the nineteenth century, their purpose and foundation remains the same, she claims, and her critique, like Dickens's before her, centers on the incompatibility of an industrial model and the human beings it aims to teach. The way we do school today, she claims, "has nothing to do with the way that actual human beings acquire knowledge."

Her book arrives at a time of growing dissatisfaction with public education across the nation. Some parents are wary of the increasingly secular environment in public schools, while others object to the standardization of the Common Core. Still others have seen their child struggle under the load of mandated testing. Not coincidentally, the last two decades have witnessed a sharp increase in alternatives. The number of public Montessori schools doubled between 2000 and 2014, and classical and charter schools have expanded at similar, if not higher, rates. Many of these schools have long waitlists.

One of the main drivers of this trend was a book Susan Wise Bauer published with her mother in 1999 called *The Well-Trained Mind: A Guide to Classical Education at Home*. A bible-cum-encyclopedia of resources ostensibly aimed at homeschoolers, the book served as a touchstone for educators who, in the intervening years, founded schools on the classical and great-books models. My wife and I, both homeschooled for portions of our childhood, reference the book frequently as we make decisions about our own children's education. Now in its fourth edition, the book gives a masterful and practical explication of the stages of the classical trivium (grammar, logic, rhetoric) and reveals the author, who herself was the subject of a homeschooling experiment, to be an authority not just on homeschooling but on K-12 education in general. Her book is the first thing I recommend to friends interested in becoming more involved in their child's education.

Rethinking School attempts to bring Wise Bauer's homeschooling wisdom to a new audience. Here she puts aside her discussion of classical education and adopts the language of modern educational professionals – learning disorders, standardized testing, multiple intelligences – to take aim at a system designed, she claims, so that "one teacher could corral and indoctrinate dozens of students at a time."

THESE ARE harsh words for an enterprise with the noble goal of providing a free education to every citizen, but Wise Bauer's broader critique resonates. The correlation between grade level and age is largely artificial, and more often than not children develop "asynchronously": it is perfectly natural, for instance, that a third-grader would read at a fifth-grade level and process math at a second-grade level. Understood this way, grades function as a straitjacket on the child's natural development. The system also prioritizes one type of learning style ("linear, a natural processor of symbols")

and personality ("compliant, organized . . . able to sit quietly"). According to Wise Bauer, the American public school system creates artificial norms which "have nothing to do with [students'] actual learning styles, joys, talents, and passions." When children discover something they love, they pursue it with an eagerness that never seems to exhaust them. I see this in the way my daughters dance around our living room all morning before their weekly dance class, and in their contented silence as they draw for hours beneath our picture window. Though they enjoy going to our local public school, their experience bears out Wise Bauer's point: the classroom often fatigues them, while their independent pursuits leave them energized.

Given the outsized influence of bureaucrats and CEOs in shaping our current educational model, it comes as no surprise that the curriculum often seems out of touch with the needs of the children it aims to instruct. Thanks to supporters like Bill Gates, whose $200 million bankrolled the development of the Common Core, Big Data now has a firm

foothold in public schools, and the American classroom resembles Dickens's satirical one perhaps now more than ever. English classes read fewer works of literature and more informational texts, and because, as Wise Bauer notes, the Common Core concerns itself with skills and not content, schools devote much more time to developing students' ability to process data than to exposing them to works of art that might move them. The many hours of required testing loom large on every teacher's calendar, and their students' performance often determines the amount of federal funding their school receives. But who is looking out for the best interests of the children? Wise Bauer rightly praises two Oklahoma teachers whose refusal to administer standardized tests led to their state cutting its required testing hours in half. The author also lets parents in on a secret: despite what administrators tell them, they always have the right to opt out of state testing.

There are, according to Wise Bauer, two ways out of the straitjacket of public education: either pull your children out of the system and educate them at home, where you can cater to

their specific learning styles and allow them to progress naturally, or "take control of the K-12 years yourself, and use your own ingenuity to bend the system to fit your child." In other words, if you're not willing to abandon public education, stretch it to its breaking point by relentlessly advocating for your children: Push to have your children diagnosed with a learning disability (it will give them an advantage). Keep logs of the time they spend on schoolwork at home (to have hard data when advocating for less homework). Are they gifted in one area? Then ask to have them accelerated in that subject without having to move up an entire grade. Advocating for your kid, it seems, is a full-time job.

As a high school teacher and parent of grade-school children, I believe that Wise Bauer is right about many of the system's problems. But her solutions are not viable. Her ideal school, it turns out, is a school of one.

Wise Bauer's ideal student comes across as an atomized unit who will suffer unless placed in a learning situation tailor-made for her unique personality and style. In my experience as an educator, the level of parent advocacy required to achieve this ideal situation harms the child in question more than it helps. Kids who are accustomed to mom or dad ironing out every perceived wrinkle in their educational experience are hamstrung whenever real adversity presents itself. Schools suffer, too,

when parents advocate so heavily for their own. Take, for example, the bitter fights that occur when affluent cities and towns (frequently in the Northeast) consider redrawing the lines for school districts. Parents whose children stand to be reassigned to lower-performing schools often organize and lobby to keep the map in their favor, even if shifts in the population necessitate changes. Gerrymandered school districts result, ensuring that the best educational resources remain the privilege of the wealthiest. The late sociologist Charles Tilly dubbed this phenomenon "opportunity hoarding."

Though she never puts it in these terms, for the author, securing an education for your child is not unlike waiting outside of the mall in the early hours of Black Friday, ready to elbow your way to the aisle that holds the scarcest, and therefore most coveted, product. If education is nothing but a consumer good, subject to the impersonal calculus of supply and demand, then she is right – every child for himself. But here Wise Bauer falls into a similar error to the architects of the factory model in the nineteenth century. Whereas they conceived of the educated student as a commodity to be efficiently produced, the author conceives of the educated student as the consumer, and the educational experience itself as the commodity to be examined, perhaps customized, and eventually, consumed. Both approaches, in starting from a consumerist mindset, cannot account for the role education plays in sustaining the larger community.

Children with parents capable and willing to advocate for them to the extent Wise Bauer suggests already have a leg up on their peers. But what about everyone else? After all, as she herself admits, the system was designed to help immigrants – those without the time, social capital, or economic resources to pull strings for their own children. Wise Bauer's solution – "flex the system to accommodate our children" – leaves the most vulnerable to fend for themselves.

Interestingly, the author does not suggest any alternatives besides homeschooling. Though she offhandedly mentions that she sent her own daughter to a Montessori school, she fails to engage it, or the classical model, at any depth. Doing so would have strengthened her project of "rethinking" public school, as these alternatives have thrived in recent years in response to the same shortcomings in K-12 education that she highlights in the book. And though Wise Bauer is not critical of public school teachers themselves, she ignores the fact that many talented and passionate ones are able to create spaces where students thrive. My daughters' experience at our local public elementary school bears this out. Though the school isn't perfect – they spend more time in front of screens there than my wife and I think healthy, for example – we have been impressed by its ability to work with, not against, its students' natural capacity for learning. In

Education is not a transaction between parties, but a process by which we are drawn out of ourselves.

her first-grade year my daughter followed the cycles of the moon; invented, wrote, and illustrated stories for her class's literary journal; and candled duck eggs expectantly until, at last, they hatched. Activities like these would have been exactly the kinds of things we would have wanted her to pursue had we decided to homeschool her. And she loved it – for several weeks our dinner table conversation consisted almost entirely of reports on how the ducks were coming along. Her experience, and those of countless others in public schools with talented teachers and administrators, serves as a challenge to Wise Bauer's blanket condemnation of the classroom *qua* system.

I N O R D E R T O participate in a larger community, the individual must sacrifice desirable things. A healthy society may debate what exactly those things should be, but, outside of Ayn Rand's most ardent disciples, very few would question whether individuals need to sacrifice them at all. Wise Bauer's book, however, presents the individual as paramount. In drawing an unnecessarily stark contrast between the child and the system, the author, perhaps unwittingly, creates an environment in which students must compete against each other for the most custom-catered academic experience.

Whether parents send their children off to school or keep them at home, they always learn in the context of a community. Even in Wise Bauer's ideal classroom of one, the student learns by encountering other ideas, and in responding to them, communicates, in a very real way, with the great minds of the past and present. The importance of community is something that my ten years as a high school English teacher have taught me. I never fail to marvel at the way in which students grow through others, whether it is a gifted one tasked with explaining a concept to a classmate who struggles, or a shy one discovering that she has something to say in a group discussion. Ultimately, my best students are the most generous and enthusiastic; they know that they are but small participants in something much greater than themselves.

One such student – I'll call him Evan – began my Humanities class as a quiet, unemotional high school sophomore who felt more at home in the hard sciences. The qualitative thinking and self-expression that the liberal arts demanded terrified him. He bristled in our class's required discussions, and when he wrote, his sentences came out in short, telegraphic chunks. Over the course of the year, however, the communal aspect of learning transformed him. In class discussion he began to challenge the ideas of others and examine his own, and he actually grew to look forward to our writing workshops. After we read and discussed essays by Walker Percy and Leo Tolstoy, Evan appeared at my office door. "I love this stuff," he told me, before asking for more reading suggestions. Though still very much an aspirant scientist, he had also grown into a searcher, concerned not just with questions of *how* we live but also *why*. His transformation serves as proof that an education is not a transaction between parties, but a process by which we are drawn out of ourselves by encountering the larger world.

ULTIMATELY, I think Wise Bauer would agree with this statement. As she makes clear in *The Well-Trained Mind* and in parts of *Rethinking School*, she genuinely believes that homeschooling provides the best opportunity for children to encounter, examine, and love the world around them. And she might be right. But the problem remains that the vast majority of Americans possess neither the connections nor the resources to advocate for their children to the extent *Rethinking School* demands, and as a result, her critique of K-12 education ignores the very population our nation's public schools were designed to serve. The American classroom may in fact be broken, but what would Wise Bauer say to those children, many of whom are immigrants, who nonetheless must huddle within its four walls? Straitjacket or not, the public school offers them their only hope for a better life. Her book is helpful in pointing out the serious flaws with a system that at times seems more attentive to the needs of Washington bureaucrats than individual children, but it does not provide solutions grounded in the common good. Let's hope such a book comes along soon. ⇒

On Praying for Your Children

JOHANN CHRISTOPH BLUMHARDT

The writings of Lutheran pastor Johann Christoph Blumhardt (1805–1880) spring from his personal experiences of the active power of God in spiritual warfare, revival, and miraculous healing. Here, he writes to a parent concerned about an errant young person.

Question: Why doesn't God answer the prayers of parents for their children to find faith?

Answer: First of all, the assumption that one's prayer is not answered is not always justified. Basically it is never justified, even if everything is in order on the part of the one praying. For the fact that an answer is not immediately seen is not yet proof that God has not answered. Thus, many a mother prays that her son may go to church more regularly, take more part in devotions at home, and show an interest in Christian concerns. But she should not think that her longing will be granted at the very next opportunity. It can take a long time for her prayers to bear fruit. Yet the Lord is already working in secret toward it. Further, prayers for the salvation of one's children cannot find an immediate answer as easily as prayers for delivery from danger or from an illness. In the latter case the Lord can act independently of the person concerned, for it depends on him alone. But for a person to turn and to actively seek his salvation, God's will alone does not suffice. Something on the part of that person is also needed.

The individual is not a machine which can be maneuvered this way and that at will; he has a free will and can say, "I do not want to." God does not wish to use force. The less inclined a person is, the more is needed on God's part to prepare that free will to become one with God's. Often a person is strongly bound by powerful inclinations and passions,

Sherrie York, *Longing,* linocut

as well as by dark influences. These bonds must be broken one by one before God's influences can take effect. This takes time. Such a person has picked up anti-Christian impulses bit by bit, and so become entangled in unbelief; to shed these impulses, to free one's spirit from everything that makes it unbelieving and profane, can require much time.

God has much work to do before the fruit of his work can be seen. But every mother who prays can believe confidently that the Lord becomes active as soon as the request comes to him in the right way. She must have patience until the fruits are shown. Years can go by before the groundwork is laid. Meantime, any afflictions her son may experience can only help the matter on. Even if the results are not fully shown in his lifetime, he can yet be put right on the deathbed. We must not regard anyone as lost so long as someone is praying for him in clear and constant concern.

However, it can also be that not everything is in order with the one praying. This may be the reason that the prayer bears so little fruit. Some people are satisfied so long as their loved ones conduct themselves decently to all appearances and do not neglect Christian conventions. If this is not the case, then they pray for them. But they do not have the highest in mind, often because they themselves are not spiritual enough, are not really in fellowship with the Lord. Then things may work out in a curious way: Here they are, praying for the spiritual well-being of their children, while they themselves do not stand rightly before God. However, even the prayers of such persons are

More is accomplished through prayer by carrying the matter quietly than by using many words.

not entirely in vain in God's eyes: he is glad whenever he is approached in prayer. Even unsuitable prayers and intercessions often make a great difference, so that redemption for eternal life takes place which perhaps would not have happened if nobody had prayed. But time must elapse and circumstances change before the full answer can be given.

Finally, I would like to say that one's prayers accomplish more if one carries a situation quietly on one's heart rather than using many words every day. In the latter case, it often looks as if one were trying to force something from God, wishing to hasten the matter on, contrary to the orderly course it may otherwise take. Then nothing can come of one's strenuous efforts.

Here, then, is the most effective way to pray for one's loved ones: Be mindful at all times that you yourself walk constantly with the Lord, and be attentive to those for whom you pray. Guard against thoughtlessness, against stupidity, harshness, and strictness, against an overbearing manner that is unfriendly and inconsiderate. Otherwise you will hinder more than you help. All these things must be kept in mind when one prays for one's relatives, and it must all take place before God. Then it may well be that the time will soon come for God's spirit to effect his cause more speedily and fully than has been apparent until now. For the Lord will one day take up his cause again in person. Until then, may he comfort all souls that are troubled about their loved ones, and fill them with patience and faith! In the end, the Lord will indeed lead everything in glory to the salvation of all souls that are commended to him. ⤳

Source: Johann Christoph Blumhardt, *Besprechung wichtiger Glaubensfragen aus der Seelsorge hervorgegangen* (Karlsruhe: Evangelischer Schriftenverein für Baden, 1888). Translated by Alan Stevenson.

Anja Percival,
Café Light XV

"We Pray God to Be Free of God"

Avid the vastness to eat everything in sight:
bone mule, dun man, westward leastward grow the trees,
even the clouds irradiated into blue.
Here in cucumber Connecticut it reaches even me,
hard land, hard light that I without seeing see.
It would be a mercy not to name it God.
It would be assent and assertion both to stand,
human, in a final light feeling nothing
but light, as from the land, and from the mind,
it fades, and cedes to even greater space.
It would be nerve and star, nowhere, near.
It would be creeping and it would be teeth.
It would be darkness, darkness, darkness.
And it would come morning.

CHRISTIAN WIMAN

Anja Percival,
Night Light VI

"Meaning Is Not Man's Gift to Reality"

Another morning of mist.
How many do I have left?
Another morning of missed.
The habit of lack is hell
to break. The German girl
had a little black abyss
between her two front teeth
that flashed – if you can imagine
blackness flashing – through everything
she said. She said,
pinning back her turbulent hair
and cheerfully chewing English
like a *sonnenblumenbrot*,
that she was "tensed"
about the poetry in my class,
since it comes – the little abyss! –
from the, how do you say,
"breath-crystal" of a language?
There had been for both of us
a boy – American, obviously,
and Midwestern, I would guess –
who raised his hand like a clean
stalk of wheat and asked
in a way that was already an answer
shouldn't an experience of God
bring us, I don't know, peace?

It rained while I was writing this.
It rained, and my father died,
and it stopped, and it rained,
and I leaned down close to a flower
for which I had no name, and it stopped,
and my great-great-granddaughter
tried to think what it might mean
to pray and it rained
and it burned and I found myself
in front of faces talking less
about connections than the seams
between things because it seems
no matter the knowledge or vision
there is this need, this void, this
mist. "The poem is lonely,"
the poet says. "It intends another
and it goes out toward her."
You come downstairs
wearing what you wear
and moving as you move
up to the glass beside me, where we see,
mostly, what we do not see:
neighbors and playthings, tree limbs
one tick past implicit.
Even the sun's in trust.

CHRISTIAN WIMAN

Gustaf
Tenggren,
*Little Red
Riding Hood*

The World Is Your Classroom

A Letter to My Granddaughter

FIDA MEIER

Walden, New York
December 2018

Dear Nancy,

This grandmother of yours has just turned eighty – a venerable age, though I don't feel different. Age is not something to be embarrassed about in spite of the physical limitations it imposes. For me it is a time of counting my blessings. Including, among many, the chance to see you, now in your early twenties, grow into full adulthood.

In thinking of your future, I realize that I *am* old – not only "getting old," as folks kindly say. Who knows if when you graduate from university I'll be able to share what is on my heart for your future? I want to do it now – not that I will

Fida Meier is a teacher who lives at Fox Hill, a Bruderhof in Walden, New York.

Gustaf
Tenggren,
*The Dragon
of the North*

a helping hand, accepts help, and remains undeterred by obstacles. Such a quest is life. The hero wins the prize by sheer generosity and goodness of heart. To win the prize you need a vision. Set out bravely, willing to endure hardships. And win companions on the way who help you gain the goal.

Like a fairy-tale companion, I have accompanied you through victorious and stressful times. Oh! The frustration of being misunderstood! That keen sense of injustice in the young! Mine was not to meddle in such trouble. My task was solely to absorb the turbulence, trusting completely in your resilient spirit to rise above conflicts. Then, to help you apply that important sense of justice to those who suffer the real injustices of the world: poverty, prejudice, and political oppression. Your grandfather Andreas – a schoolteacher who, like me, had grown up in the backwoods of Paraguay – sought to implant a sense of Jesus' preference for the poor, endangered, downtrodden into every student he taught.

I have seen your character grow, and your sense of yourself. We can sometimes feel our identities are threatened when others confront us with criticism. But self-perspective is never perfect; the objectivity of others can actually hone our best qualities, not threaten or destroy them.

With the unknown future before you, there is always a question of where to invest your talents. It amazes me that you embraced the challenge to study in my old home of Montevideo, Uruguay, after growing up here in the United States. Just think of what your studies will enable you to read! You can read

always hit the mark. But you grandchildren have always been forgiving about your Oma's rambling. I marvel at this bond between us that enables me to share my thoughts with you based on my own struggles and experiences across generations, space, and time. I'm sure they do not always match your present situation, yet I hope you can glean from them some useful truth.

I've always been a storyteller, like my own Nona was to me, and I firmly believe in fairy tales. They almost always depict the fight between good and evil, giving insights into human avarice, ambition, hardheartedness. It is not the rich, the clever, or the strong who slay dragons, but the honest one who gives

Jorge Luis Borges with his eloquent mastery of words, Gabriel García Marquez's *One Hundred Years of Solitude* in the original language, the voice of all the world's exiles in the poems of Julia Esquivel. And you can appreciate authors like Cormac McCarthy, who grafted Spanish phrases so hauntingly into *All the Pretty Horses*.

Yet there is not only the question of language, but of your identity. The pressure to conform in any college setting is intense, be it in dress, music, or the party scene. To choose your own way of expressing your identity, when it goes against the norm, costs something. How important, then, to seek common ground wherever possible. I'm so glad to know you are having a good time without sacrificing inner values. Yes, you've had to face criticism of your country. What happens in the United States makes a splash across the world. Yet if you truly love your country, you'll want to know how it is viewed from afar. It will strengthen your resolve to work for its betterment. Friends and foes can sharpen your awareness of its strengths and its weaknesses. The same goes for the small Bruderhof community in which you grew up.

Now in a new continent, you'll be finding yourself probing much you hadn't questioned before. Your faith in God the Creator and in Christ your Savior has been put into the crucible many times in these past years. Reason wants to fit faith into the capacity of our brains. Alas! How small a god would God be if that could be the case? The apostle Paul speaks in such glorious terms of faith as believing in the realities we don't see! Even science admits many of such mysteries. You can take a flower apart, name each part, but never assemble it again into a living plant.

Like that living flower with its many parts, you are also part of a greater, mysterious whole: not only part of a family or community, not only part of a nation, but part of the fabric of humanity woven by God. Yours is a particular strand called to be in harmony with the great pattern of redemption: restoring this earth to its original purpose in the vast universe, that of serving and honoring its Creator, healing its broken relationships, and righting the injustices of society that put the weak and the poor at risk – not to mention the environment. All your capacities are to be employed to achieve that goal. The challenge is to invest not only your intellect, but your whole self into that service! The key to that challenge is in the Gospels. It was implanted by God into human hearts from of old: "Love your neighbor as yourself."

I hope I'll still be around when you come home. Then life's lessons will truly begin. Self-expression through your gifts is a natural urge. But it is not the ultimate goal. Harmony is! At work, you'll be part of a team with the same goals you've been striving for. Even so, character differences might cause you frustrations, especially when other opinions seem to hamper or limit your creativity. Yet be willing to see a conflict through your coworkers' eyes. Taking the first step toward reconciliation demands humility and courage. Remember you are on a quest for something higher than self-fulfillment: "Seek ye first the kingdom of God" and "Blessed are those who hunger and thirst for righteousness" are the most important guidelines. Real life can get messy, and sometimes you'll need to find the humility to sacrifice your own best-laid plans. But the goal you work for is greater than your own satisfaction.

Of course any work, even work you love,

> **Self-perspective is never perfect; the objectivity of others can hone our best qualities.**

can become repetitive and wearing. So how do you keep up your vibrancy of spirit? Maintaining relationships beyond the work place is still very important. Seek out not only like-minded company, but also folks with other reactions to the subjects that preoccupy you that day. They may add to your understanding of cause and effect, or outline your own conviction more sharply. Indifference, self-preoccupation – even hostility to something or someone unknown is hard to conquer and so prevalent in the young. Trying to understand where it comes from helps to bridge the gap. And seek out the old, not only the young. They can be mentors to you: true friends who dare to tell you where you are wrong without fear of ruining the relationship.

> **Because it takes time, real reading penetrates your inner being.**

And read! Save time each day for reading. In high school you read the great American classics: *The Grapes of Wrath*, *The Great Gatsby*, Chaim Potok's *The Chosen*. When I read them as a teen, I read solely for the plot, the intensity of human emotions, and their tumult and ecstasies beyond my personal experience. Only as an adult was I startled and profoundly moved by their lessons. So keep on reading widely and deeply.

There is a surfeit of propaganda, slogans, and information that assault our senses continuously today. But real reading, because it takes time, affects you quite differently. It penetrates your inner being. I personally like fiction, historical fiction in particular. As Rabbi Shalom Carmy, a professor of philosophy at Yeshiva University, writes:

> History books cannot replace novels. We read Dickens or George Eliot because these writers

have a vision and an insight. They show us new and striking perspectives on the world, bringing to the fore aspects often invisible in the works of nonfiction. They articulate a profound understanding of human nature, illuminating the often obscure motives and reasoning that guides our behavior. They give us something we cannot get from a social scientist, historian, or journalist.

History, if it's merely a string of facts, is blind to the human soul. But to see history through the eyes of those who lived it will bring our common humanity alive. This is what helps me remember historical facts to this day: Alan Paton's *Cry, the Beloved Country*, Julia Alvarez's *In the Time of the Butterflies*, and Markus Zusak's *The Book Thief* are recent ones, but of course Hemmingway's *A Farewell to Arms* and *For Whom the Bell Tolls*, and Herman Wouk's *The Winds of War* belong to our country's classics. I do like positive endings (not necessarily happy ones) in which conflict is faced and comes to some humanly possible – if not divine – resolution. Don't we all hope for a measure of redemption in every conflict, personally, yes, and publicly?

There will be times ahead when you will feel empty, tasked beyond your strength. These times are part of life's circle. Endure them, trusting that God will fill you again both with inspiration and inner energy. And there will be times when God places a "no" in your path that is hard to understand. Embracing it will give you amazing insights into his plan for you. Once when I was in a time of inner crisis, a dear friend of mine wrote to me that the stones God seemingly places in our path are placed there not to hinder us, but to make us stop and consider whether we are traveling in the right direction – or whether maybe we should turn back and start over.

Here's one more thought that may seem mundane but can help bring unexpected joy. Although you have a specific training and skills, living in community requires the involvement of your whole self, not only your professional self. That might mean looking after an elderly person – easing her struggle with dependence by your cheerful spirit, and perhaps gaining a mentor in the process. Or it might mean embracing something you do not wish to do, even something you think you cannot do. The results may surprise you! As you know, I taught school for many years. Teaching was my passion: to accompany a child through hurdles to success was my joy in life. Imagine my disorientation when, as a young mother many years ago, circumstances led me to change jobs and I suddenly found myself responsible for a team of seamstresses. I didn't know how to sew, and wept bitterly over the loss of my daily involvement with the children. I was sure everyone soon would see how incapable I was of my new task.

But guess what? The women I worked with had much more patience with me than I ever had with myself. Bit by bit I learned that skill – one that now makes it possible for me, at age eighty, to go each day to our community's workshop to sew upholstery for the wonderful furniture we build. (Not to mention sewing gifts and toys for friends and grandchildren too.) That I'm still able to contribute in this way gives me great satisfaction. When we let others trust us to succeed in something new, we may discover talents we had never suspected in ourselves.

What's more, this experience didn't spell the end of my work as an educator, but broadened and enriched it. In the decades since, the chance to accompany children and young

people in all kinds of situations, as a teacher, mentor, and grandmother, has been a great blessing for my own life. Trust is a precious gift that I never take for granted, whether offered by the young – like you, my dear – or by the old.

I mentioned your grandfather Andreas, from whom I learned so much. He only had nine years of formal schooling. But because he loved life and loved people, the world was his classroom. It can be yours as well.

This is more than enough for one letter. Now go to your favorite park in the beautiful city of Montevideo, take a good book, and enjoy some *yerba mate* for me.

With much love,

your fond Oma

Gustaf Tenggren, *The Castle in the Valley*

Paweł Kuczyński, *Passion*

The Good Reader

KAREN SWALLOW PRIOR

R EADING VIRTUOUSLY means, first, reading closely, being faithful to both text and context, interpreting accurately and insightfully. Indeed, there is something in the very form of reading – the shape of the action itself – that tends toward virtue. The attentiveness necessary for deep reading (the kind of reading we practice in reading literary works as opposed to skimming news stories or reading instructions) requires patience. The skills of interpretation and

evaluation require prudence. Even the simple decision to set aside time to read in a world rife with so many other choices competing for our attention requires a kind of temperance.

If, like me, you have lived long enough to have experienced life – and reading – before the internet, perhaps you have now found your attention span shortened and your ability to sit and read for an hour (or more) nil. The effects on our minds of the disjointed, fragmentary, and addictive nature of the digitized

Karen Swallow Prior is a professor of English at Liberty University, and is the author of several books, including On Reading Well: Finding the Good Life through Great Books *(Brazos, a division of Baker Publishing Group, 2018), from which this excerpt is taken. Used by permission.* bakerpublishinggroup.com

Paweł Kuczyński, *Snowman*

world – and the demands of its dinging, beeping, and flashing devices – are well documented. Nicholas Carr explains in *The Shallows: What the Internet Is Doing to Our Brains* that "the linear mind is being pushed aside by a new kind of mind that wants and needs to take in and dole out information in short, disjointed, often overlapping bursts – the faster, the better." Our brains work one way when trained to read in logical, linear patterns, and another way when continually bouncing from tweet to tweet, picture to picture, and screen to screen. These effects on the brain are amplified by technology developers who intentionally build addictive qualities into programs in order to increase user engagement, as some industry leaders have acknowledged. Whether you feel you have lost your ability to read well, or you never acquired that ability at all, be encouraged. The skills required to read well are no great mystery. Reading well is, well, simple (if not easy). It just takes time and attention.

Reading well begins with understanding the words on the page. In nearly three decades

Polish artist Paweł Kuczyński studied at the Academy of Fine Arts in Poznan and is an internationally recognized satirical cartoonist. See more of his work at plough.com/surrealtimes.

Paweł Kuczyński, *Big Baby*

of teaching literature, I've noticed that many readers have been conditioned to jump so quickly to interpretation and evaluation that they often skip the fundamental but essential task of comprehending what the words actually mean. This habit of the mind can be seen in the body. When I ask students to describe or restate a line or passage, often their first response is to turn their eyes upward in search of a thought or an idea, rather than to look down at the words on the page in front of them where the answer actually lies. Attending to

the words on the page requires deliberation, and this improves with practice.

P RACTICE MAKES PERFECT, but pleasure makes practice more likely, so read something enjoyable. If a book is so agonizing that you avoid reading it, put it down and pick up one that brings you pleasure. Life is too short and books are too plentiful not to. Besides, one can't read well without enjoying reading.

Paweł Kuczyński, *TV and Books*

On the other hand, the greatest pleasures are those born of labor and investment. A book that requires nothing from you might offer the same diversion as that of a television sitcom, but it is unlikely to provide intellectual, aesthetic, or spiritual rewards long after the cover is closed. Therefore, even as you seek books that you will enjoy reading, demand ones that make demands on you: books with sentences so exquisitely crafted that they must be reread, familiar words used in fresh ways, new words so evocative that you are compelled to look them up, and images and ideas so arresting that they return to you unbidden for days to come.

Also, read slowly. Just as a fine meal should be savored, so, too, good books are to be luxuriated in, not rushed through. Certainly, some reading material merits a quick read, but habitual skimming is for the mind what a steady diet of fast food is for the body. Speed-reading is not only inferior to deep reading but may bring more harm than benefits: one critic cautions that reading fast is simply a "way of

Paweł Kuczyński, *Blacksmith*

Paweł Kuczyński, *Pearl*

fooling yourself into thinking you're learning something." When you read quickly, you aren't thinking critically or making connections. Worse yet, "speed-reading gives you two things that should never mix: superficial knowledge and overconfidence." Don't be discouraged if you read slowly. Thoughtfully engaging with a text takes time. The slowest readers are often the best readers, the ones who get the most meaning out of a work and are affected most deeply by literature. Seventeenth-century Puritan divine Richard

Baxter writes, "It is not the reading of many books which is necessary to make a man wise or good; but the well reading of a few, could he be sure to have the best."

Read with a pen, pencil, or highlighter in hand, marking in the book or taking notes on paper. The idea that books should not be written in is an unfortunate holdover from grade school, a canard rooted in a misunderstanding of what makes a book valuable. The true worth of books is in their words and ideas, not their pristine pages. ⤳

EUGENE VODOLAZKIN

Kindergarten

A Personal History

Translated from the Russian by Anya Migdal

WE OWE THE NAME of this institution to the German pedagogue Friedrich Wilhelm August Froebel, but the very first kindergarten was established long before him by Robert Owen. This was the same Owen whom older Russian generations remember from their compulsory studies of scientific communism. Even those who justly considered communism unscientific knew it was from Owen specifically that Marx borrowed a number of absurdities which laid the foundation of his

Eugene Vodolazkin is the author of several acclaimed novels, including Laurus *and* The Aviator. *He lives in Saint Petersburg, Russia.*

theory of communism.

Time spent in kindergarten varies from country to country. In the US, I'm told, it's only a year. In the USSR, kindergarten lasted for four hopeless years. When I found myself there at the age of three, I must admit I didn't know much about Froebel or Owen, but the very idea of gathering people in an enclosed space was already repulsive to me. "Young Pioneer" summer camps, other types of militarized assembly – none of those warmed my heart. Even less joy was evoked by the collectivization of labor – from making snowmen to grownup large-scale tasks.

It's not that I have anything against large-scale tasks. It's rather that I felt (and still do) that they ought to be solved by individual effort. One could argue that some tasks may only be solved by a group – such as the creation of a *very large* snowman. Here I'll have to agree. It's true, making a very large snowman is hard to do alone. But perhaps such a snowman is simply not necessary.

In years past there used to be more snow; in my kindergarten days we were always rolling giant balls of snow and pushing them in groups of three or four. That's when I grasped what it means for something "to snowball." The round mass we pushed would devour fallen snow with a crunch, leaving behind uneven tracks, black from last year's foliage. The subsequent problem was that we couldn't manage placing one of these giant snowballs on top of another. This was the punishment for our megalomania. We reminded ourselves of Robinson Crusoe, who, having hollowed out a tree trunk to make a canoe, was unable to drag it to the water. Our monster globs would last until the end of winter, and out of everything snowy in our garden they melted last.

If I'm being precise, I should say that I went to two different kindergartens, not one. The

first one is a little fuzzy in my memory, due to my tender age. All I have left from this period, with few exceptions, is this quatrain:

> *That is Lenin in that portrait*
> *In a frame with leaves of green*
> *He was glorious but simple*
> *Just the best the world had seen.*

It could come as a surprise that out of all the *twinkle-twinkles*, this specific rhyme stuck in my head, but then again, what would be so surprising about that? Zombification in the USSR began in the womb. These lines clung to my memory with "In a frame with leaves of green." The directness of childhood perception could not reconcile this puzzling frame with the one I actually saw – our kindergarten's Lenin was housed in a simple wooden rectangle. For some years I tried to find an acceptable explanation for these curious lines, by mentally relocating the action to the jungle, say, until coming to the realization that other rhymed assertions had been even more dubious.

Two kindergartens conflated in my memory into one, so I don't see anything wrong with combining them in this narrative. The second kindergarten here engulfs the first, but it has every right to do so. *This* kindergarten corresponded to its name fully, for children there spent their time in an honest-to-goodness garden.

In order to find it one had to duck into a courtyard from the street, and upon reaching one of the building entryways, to walk up to the second floor. A simple apartment door opened into the kindergarten. The building was situated on top of a small hill that was hard to make out in the city landscape. However, even while obscured by buildings, the hill remained, continuing its mysterious existence. It opened up only to those who, having climbed up to

Photographs public domain

the second floor, exited the other side. Here the second floor became the first floor. And that's where the entrance to the garden was found.

This garden, if memory serves, was planted with fruit, and it had acacia trees lining its perimeter. It continued picking up altitude with the hill, but because it was near the top, the climb wasn't very noticeable. At least I don't remember movement throughout the garden registering as movement up and down. It was here that we made snowmen in the winter. In summer we had other pastimes.

Duels, for instance. Or more precisely, the same duel, acted out over and over – the one between Onegin and Lensky. The cast was invariable: me, and some other boy whose name I no longer remember. We had seen the opera *Eugene Onegin* with our parents and were both shaken to our cores. The romantic collision left us indifferent, but that bodeful "Now advance!" left an indelible impression on us both. In this dueling scene I was cast, in keeping with my name, as Onegin, and my buddy (perhaps he was a Vladimir?) as Lensky.

This presumed Vladimir was quite rotund and after my gunshot he'd fall rather awkwardly. He exercised caution, choosing a good spot on the grass while slapping his thigh for some reason. I kept showing him how it ought to be done, kept explaining that he can't choose where to fall, but it was all futile. Swaying on his half-bent legs, he'd touch the ground with his hand and only then would he fall on his side, twigs crackling underneath.

I discovered the romantic side of *Eugene Onegin*, as well as the magical music of this opera, after kindergarten. I was given a record and listened to it a lot, probably more times than I'd dueled with Lensky. Having memorized all the arias I would sing them to the best of my (modest) abilities. And even now, when I listen to something from time to time

(although I no longer duel) after a couple of drinks at an intimate gathering I'm still able to belt out something or other. I'm not at all sure that my singing pleases my friends, but that's what friends are for – to make certain sacrifices. The roots of my dubious vocal prowess go back, unquestionably, to my opera-inspired duels.

I should note that these duels belong to the later period of my kindergarten days. This was the high note – a high F, so to say, of my existence before school. Yet it began in a much more modest way: the first two years of kindergarten were the main source of my childhood sorrows. Nobody was mean to me, but my unwillingness to go there could be likened to a fear of going to the dentist. Furthermore, in rating my reluctance, the dentist would, I think, win out over the kindergarten because the former was just a normal fear of pain – there was no dental anesthesia back then – while the latter was an insurmountable despair, inexplicable to all, including me.

The first two years of kindergarten were the main source of my childhood sorrows.

It should be noted that my behavior, too, was irrational. I would obediently get up, wash up, allow myself to be dressed in a shirt and baggy pants (I still remember the winter version of these) and would rather calmly proceed all the way up to the kindergarten door. Once there, I would abruptly turn around and continue walking – in the opposite direction. When they'd bring me back I would begin to sob and beg them not to leave me in this sad, sad place.

Everyone who got to accompany me to kindergarten was astounded by the fact that I began my maneuvers specifically upon reaching the door. They didn't ask me about it directly (the very question would have hinted at the acceptability of the action) but rather indirectly would pry as to why my tantrums unfailingly began at the very last moment, instead of while I was washing or having those baggy pants pulled up my legs. After all, I was aware of the destination from the get-go.

What could I answer? Yes, obviously I knew where we were going, and would begin moping upon waking, having barely opened my eyes. Generally speaking, mornings were a rather cheerless affair for me. Gloomy darkness outside my window, plastic-sounding voices coming from an old radio – none of it improved my mood. But I was at home, and in gratitude for this I was willing to look out into the snowy gloom, to listen to the radio, and God knows what else I was willing to do! Before we reach my kindergarten door, thought I, so much could still happen. So a terminally ill patient refuses to poison what's left of his time with histrionics.

I was able to control my sorrow even as we walked down the street. Stretching what was left of my minutes into eternity, I would tell myself that we still had a long way to go: first we'll have to walk past the pharmacy, past some sort of bronze fellow on a horse, past the thorny bushes. Walking by the bushes I thought about how we still have to duck into the courtyard and then walk up to the second floor. And on the second floor is where, obviously, it would all begin.

When they'd ask me why I cried so much approaching the classroom I'd answer that the lamps were too bright. From the view of the grownups, lighting could not be a serious cause for suffering, and so no changes were ever made. Had I invented something like an inability to get along with the kids (or teachers) in class, my complaints would probably have been met with more empathy. But I was telling the honest (although improbable) truth: nothing brought me more despair than the piercing light of the fluorescent bulbs. These noxious rays were completely unlike the soft lighting at my house. They mercilessly illuminated the shortcomings of this preschool institution (primarily, the presence of wicked and energetic children) that, presumably, under different lighting conditions, would have been left in the shadows.

Any change to my established world order brought with it a new wave of unhappiness, and so it was a true shock to the system when the dining tables were swapped. One fine morning, instead of our comfortable – albeit somewhat worn – dining tables, the pupils of the kindergarten discovered long-legged monsters of an unnaturally yellow color. At home I recounted how sitting at these tables it was impossible to reach one's food, and suggested not going to kindergarten anymore. This sounded even less plausible than the story of the light bulbs, so back to kindergarten I went.

But the next morning, to my great surprise, the legs of the tables had already been shortened (with the sawed-off bits carefully stacked in the corner). The tables themselves had been lowered to an appropriate height and the dishes from the school kitchen were once again within arm's reach. The cuisine didn't bring much joy, but the return of the tables to a familiar size had a calming effect on me.

A teachable moment: little humans do not like changes. They like it when today is exactly like yesterday, and tomorrow is like today. That's why, for example, one shouldn't travel too much with them. Frequent trips tire them out. I also think they don't so much like reading as they enjoy re-reading, because that is a return to the familiar.

But back to the aforementioned cuisine. This is a separate conversation, and thinking about that food still makes me hiccup. Clumpy semolina porridge, red bars of alleged beets in the borsch, pasta with a chlorine smell, rubbery pears in compote – the menu wasn't terribly varied. Keeping down these delicacies was a task failed by many. I can still hear the despondent bickering with our teacher about how much we must eat and how much we could leave on the plate.

Remembering all this, I had many doubts about sending my own daughter to kindergarten. And having sent her, I was anticipating the same suffering and laments. I was ready to take her out at the first sign of trouble, to finally say out loud all that was left unsaid in childhood, to put a curse upon this institution for eternity. But to my great surprise, my daughter liked going to kindergarten, even growing upset when I'd pick her up early. This wasn't the same kindergarten I went to, but they are all so similar. None of them would have suited me.

My childhood suffering subsided in time. Something happened (they say I grew out of it) and by five and a half I went to kindergarten not without joy. The food, of course, hadn't improved and I rarely ate there (I was allowed breakfast at home) but it wasn't food that had been the bane of my kindergarten existence. I no longer sank into a depression at the thought of having to go there, of spending time with, among others, those I didn't like. Any kind of accidental – and perhaps involuntary – assembly presumes that you'll have to spend time with those you'd otherwise avoid. It also implies a fixed hierarchy when instead one wants to presume every person unique, existing outside of any constructs.

In that second, happy period of my kindergarten life, all was well with my place in the hierarchy. I had the opportunity to duel to my heart's content (and this required a rather high degree of freedom) and to do whatever is normally available to one with rights. Furthermore, I interpreted the scope of what was permissible to mean more, in a sense, than the other kindergarteners.

For instance, I felt free to do impressions of the employees of my kindergarten, up to (oh, the horror!) its director, Ada Georgievna. My portrayal of Ada Georgievna focused on the manner in which she ate, or more specifically, on the array of pneumonic effects that accompanied her consumption of liquids. The success of my theatrics was guaranteed because everyone knew what she did: for some reason the teachers and the director ate with the children.

Keeping down these delicacies was a task failed by many.

I should note that encouragement of my impressions didn't end with the other students: there were appreciative audience members among the teachers. Like all normal folk, the teachers didn't like their higher-ups, perhaps even despising them wholeheartedly. When Ada Georgievna was out of the room, they'd ask me to show them how she ate her pickled cucumber soup, or how she drank hot milk, and I'd oblige. Judging by their uproarious laughter, my performance wasn't half bad – especially in the soup number, which included a supposed suctioning up of not just liquid, but pickles too.

Kindergarten was a miniature model of real life, where days of glory and success intertwined with periods of failure and bad luck. One Defender of the Fatherland Day (a Soviet holiday celebrated on the twenty-third of February) our kindergarten society was paid a visit by soldiers from a nearby military unit. They told us of their difficult lives and asked about our, also difficult, lives. Somehow it came to be known that my buddy Alesha Semenov's birthday happened to be the twenty-third of February. And then Alesha got a birthday surprise: he was placed on a chair, and two of the tallest soldiers lifted him – in the chair – right up to the ceiling. He sat there, right under the plaster, holding on firmly with both hands, fear mixing with pure and utter joy in his eyes. Alesha looked down at us from above and we stood around him, tiny – even tinier than usual. And then, in the hopes of also being lifted up in the chair, I yelled out that my birthday is the twenty-first of February. Of course I didn't expect to be lifted as high as Alesha – after all, the date wasn't quite right. But on the other hand it was a small differ-ence, and practically speaking, the twenty-first is almost like the twenty-third, so surely they could have lifted me to at least half of where they lifted Alesha.

But they didn't – I never even left the ground. I was told that *almost* doesn't count, and this sounded like the voice of justice. It wasn't voiced by the soldiers; they were nice guys, and lifting up another birthday boy would have been no trouble. If I'm not mistaken, the voice belonged to the oldest employee of our kinder-garten institution, one who would periodically utter wise but utterly vicious things. And so my wings were stepped on, and happiness, having

been so near, remained just out of reach.

This missed opportunity to soar toward the ceiling became one of the biggest disappointments of my childhood, a bigger disappointment being only my unrealized dream of sailing on the leaf of a tropical plant called the *Victoria amazonica*. I had read somewhere that its leaf can hold up to twenty-five kilos and so, allegedly, children in the tropics use them as boats. I dreamed about this for a long time – until I was in second or third grade, woefully aware of my unrelenting growth and subsequent weight gain. And then my horizons expanded, life became more colorful, and the dream dissipated all by itself.

Concluding this story, I should tell you that despite an abundance of apples, my kindergarten was not a Garden of Eden. But in the manner in which its doors clanked behind me for the final time, an unexpected parallel emerged with the Pearly Gates. I was no longer allowed inside this garden. I couldn't even see it from behind the building, the fence, and the acacias. It seems to me that having been banished from paradise, Adam and Eve suffered not just because life was good there and bad outside, but also from the realization that there was no way back.

Painful is the knowledge that you can't return somewhere or that you can't return something: it's a scourge of time and space. A scourge, more immediately, in the form of bags under your eyes, a belly bulging over your belt, and, in a wider sense, in the form of experience – that is, all things that grow whether we want them to or not. I haven't checked my weight in quite a while, but I'm pretty sure it's more than twenty-five kilos. Clearly, the *Victoria amazonica* will have to set sail without me. ✎

ANDREW BALIO

Orchestras of Change

The promise of El Sistema for children from Brazil to Baltimore

Every winter – or summer, depending on your hemisphere's perspective – Campos de Jordão, a resort town in Brazil, hosts a youth orchestra camp. When I taught there, I met music students who had been sent to the program from countries across Latin America. At the end of each week of rehearsals and master classes, the orchestra would pile into the local club, whose DJ spun pop music from across the continent for the young travelers.

During the week, the kids would treat me with formality: I was one of their *maestros*. At the club, I got to see them simply enjoying themselves. Suddenly, the boys were twirling the girls around the dance floor. It was a dance-off for the sake of fun, national pride, and international courtship.

Many of these students were trained in their own countries in programs inspired by Venezuela's national musical education program. El Sistema consists of a vast network

An El Sistema performance in Göteborg, Sweden

Andrew Balio is the Principal Trumpet of the Baltimore Symphony Orchestra and founder of the Future Symphony Institute, a research body for the sustainability of classical music. futuresymphony.org

to polyphony – music in which independent voices are joined with one another in an ordered harmony. From this evolved what we know today as *classical music:* a vast body of work unique in human history for its ability to involve many people at once in ever greater musical complexity. The music taught by El Sistema trains children to live in harmony with themselves and others, achieving a formation of the whole person of which the Franciscan nuns who taught Abreu would surely approve. Playing music is about expressing something bigger than just oneself – to play is to *lose* oneself, in fact, in the beauty that answers truth and goodness.

Of course, Abreu's mission wasn't avowedly religious. At first, his goal was merely to counter-balance the solitude of the practice room by forming ensembles of anyone who desired to play. "From my very first days at the conservatory," he said, "I felt as though I had come up against a big wall. . . . One had to study alone for many years . . . and even then, the possibility of playing in an orchestra was a myth." In the face of this solitude and discouragement, Abreu wanted to build a community of music.

Soon, those impromptu garage rehearsals grew, drawing not only music students but untrained kids as well. Rather than turn them away, Abreu trained them in an improvised, epic boot camp, often working for twelve hours a day, embedding the novices among those who could actually play their parts. This was the very opposite of the customary "go home and practice" ethos that segmented players by level of ability. In fact, he didn't even hold auditions.

And then the government took notice, and soon Abreu's come-one-come-all garage orchestra was a national program. The benefit

of neighborhood music groups, called *núcleos,* which teach music to the children of the poorest of the poor as a way of plucking them from the awaiting jaws of gang membership, drugs, and broken homes. Its results have been extraordinary.

El Sistema began in 1975 as an eleven-piece garage band. Its musicians had answered the invitation of conductor José Abreu to get together to play Mozart, Vivaldi, Bach, and Handel. A polymath, Abreu was simultaneously studying petroleum economics at Andrés Bello Catholic University and learning piano, organ, and composition at the National Conservatory. When he was young, he'd studied at a music school founded by Franciscan nuns. The expert and loving training Abreu received there was deeply influential in what he created through El Sistema.

The Catholic Church, whose primary mission is to save souls, is also the wellspring from which classical music flowed. First came chant, whose modal overtones echoing in the vaults of Europe's cathedrals gave birth of the program is not limited to those who make it big, or to those who are the best players. Music making itself is good for those who do it, however limited they are in skill. Abreu was transfixed by what happens to people when they are playing classical music together; he explained: "Music has to be recognized as an agent of social development in the highest sense because it transmits the highest values – solidarity, harmony, mutual compassion." Today, Abreu's model of music instruction for the poorest children has been replicated around the world.

Flute students from the OrchKids program

A mong these spinoffs is the one in my own backyard: the Baltimore Symphony Orchestra's OrchKids program. In a school just ten blocks to the west of our home, after school, local musicians mentor kids from some of Baltimore's most impoverished neighborhoods. They learn the skills of music performance, of collaboration; they are brought into the world of classical music: into its traditions, exacting demands, and rich rewards.

I'm a trumpeter with the BSO. I play music for a living solely because I showed up for sixth grade band, along with hundreds of others on the first day of school, and was assigned a rusty cornet. That was how it worked in most American public schools when I was growing up – before budget cuts and, later, the exclusive focus on "marketable" subjects relegated classical music training only to schools in the most desirable ZIP codes. Recently, when I gave a master class through OrchKids, I found myself coaching kids struggling with

recalcitrant trumpets just as I had at their age in Wisconsin. Abreu's Venezuelan program is giving back to the United States what our own public school system has allowed to wither: classical music for all, classical music as a road out of poverty, as a community for those who need it most.

After World War II, Venezuela enjoyed great wealth generated by its oil fields and manufacturing, but it also suffered marked social divides. Today, in the midst of unprecedented economic and political crises following the drawn-out collapse of its socialist government and all manner of shortages and civil unrest, funding for everything is in question. El Sistema, launched between the boom and bust cycles as classical music for the sake of itself, has had to navigate seven different governments. It has retained funding in large part because of the political value it has had for each subsequent government. Officially nonpartisan, it has nevertheless become a political football. The current president, Nicolás Maduro, successor to Hugo Chávez, claims it as a feather in his own regime's cap, a testimony to his

secure the violinist's release.

In retribution, President Maduro cancelled two upcoming international tours that the Sistema-trained Venezuelan national youth orchestra was to have made under Dudamel's direction. "Welcome to politics, Mr. Dudamel," he said, accusing him of bringing partisanship to the previously apolitical music program.

Despite these difficulties, El Sistema carries on. More than one million young musicians have passed through the original Venezuelan program. A few, such as Dudamel, have ascended to the very heights of their profession. El Sistema is a formidable institution, and the considerable number of graduates who have succeeded can be attributed at least in part to the sheer numbers of students, rather than the application of a rigid academic methodology.

Today, Abreu's classical music training community has spawned hundreds of similar programs worldwide, and a network of music educators. These institutions have shaped the lives of millions of children – especially the poor ones whose environments are often the most devoid of clear paths to the good life. The result has been nothing short of a children's musical renaissance at a time when it seemed the leviathan of modern life would swallow up classical music whole. Each year, as I meet and teach young people at Campos de Jordão, I am newly amazed at the power of El Sistema. As Gustavo Dudamel wrote in a May 2017 statement, "The only weapons that can be given to people are the necessary tools to forge their future: books, brushes, musical instruments; in short, those that embody the highest values of the human spirit: good, truth, and beauty." ➤

A violin student from an El Sistema program in Cleveland

legitimacy. In the spring of 2017, this narrative began to fracture. In May, an eighteen-year-old violist, Armando Cañizales, was killed by Maduro's security forces at a demonstration. The program's most famous graduate, Los Angeles Philharmonic conductor Gustavo Dudamel, spoke out against the regime: "Nothing justifies bloodshed. We must stop ignoring the just cry of the people suffocated by an intolerable crisis. . . . No ideology can go beyond the common good." A few days later, Cañizales's friend, Sistema-trained twenty-four-year-old violinist Wuilly Arteaga, was arrested by the National Guard and imprisoned for playing the Venezuelan national anthem in the middle of another demonstration. His violin destroyed, he was taken to prison and tortured. Dudamel became involved in talks to

Julian Peters is an illustrator and comic book artist living in Montreal, Canada, who focuses on adapting classical poems into graphic art. julianpeterscomics.com

FOR HE HAD GONE ALONE INTO THE ISLAND

AND BROUGHT BACK THE WHOLE THING.

THE HOUSE THROBBED LIKE HIS FULL VIOLIN.

SO WHETHER HE CALLS IT SPIRIT MUSIC

OR NOT, I DON'T CARE. HE TOOK IT

OUT OF WIND OFF MID-ATLANTIC.

THE END

Editors' Picks

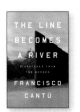

The Line Becomes a River: Dispatches from the Border
Francisco Cantú
(Riverhead)

Dispassionate analysis and hard data have their place; so does activist passion. But for a topic as politically fraught as US–Mexico border policy, it may take true stories told with honesty and intimate knowledge to bring something closer to true understanding. Few are as well-suited for this task as Francisco Cantú, a native of the Southwest who served four years in the US Border Patrol, tracking human beings across blistering deserts and bringing them in, dead or alive.

The grandson of a Mexican, Cantú tries to treat border crossers with dignity and not think too much about what happens to them after they are deported. But his idealism wears thin fast and the intense stress of the job starts to plague his dreams. Particularly affecting are his accounts of drug cartel brutality south of the border and human trafficking north of it, in which smugglers abandon stragglers and hold migrants for ransom by their impoverished relatives.

After leaving the Patrol, Cantú gets a taste of the flip side of the immigration system when he is unable to prevent the deportation of a friend who has worked undocumented in the United States for thirty years. Cantú's rare gift is an ability to evoke empathy for everyone caught up in this tragic situation – both those tasked with policing the border and those driven to risk their lives in the crossing. Such compassion in itself doesn't solve the knotty question of what to do about mass migration, a reality that is roiling politics worldwide. But it's the only good starting place in the search for a way forward.

Virgil Wander
Leif Enger
(Grove Atlantic)

In recent years nonfiction book sales have outpaced fiction. This is regrettable, and Enger's third novel shows why. Mistakenly billed as escapist literature in a time of troubling reality, it inhabits a world that can show us much about our own.

Enger captures the spirit and pathos – not to mention the linguistic and cultural quirks – of a very specific place: a hard-luck, going-nowhere Minnesota town on the shores of Lake Superior (literary territory a little north of Lake Wobegon, one reviewer has already quipped). Yet this isn't just another literary window into the heartland. Apart from its exceptionally bad weather, fictional Greenstone could be any town left behind by industry, and you may well recognize some of his characters in your own high school yearbook.

While Virgil Wander may not match Enger's 2001 bestseller, *Peace Like a River,* the Minnesotan author can still cast a magical realist spell. It only takes a pinch of the miraculous, after all, to bring lonely people together in community (of sorts) and to give their lives meaning enough to carry on.

One Person, No Vote: How Voter Suppression Is Destroying Our Democracy
Carol Anderson
(Bloomsbury)

Old Jim Crow is back in a new guise, according to this new book. Carol Anderson, a historian, paints a troubling portrait of US democracy today: in at least twenty-four states, being poor, black, Native

American, elderly, or young can make you an intended target of various "voter suppression" tactics enacted by state and local governments for partisan purposes.

An equal right to vote was not, of course, enshrined in the original US Constitution. But since the country's founding, it's a right that many have fought and died to earn. So what went wrong? In Anderson's telling, in 2013 the Supreme Court's *Shelby v. Holder* ruling dismantled key provisions of the 1965 Voting Rights Act, the landmark victory of the civil rights movement. Since then, states have passed a flurry of new laws with the stated goal of stamping out voter fraud. Yet one large survey found only thirty-one instances of fraud in over a billion votes cast. Looking behind the scenes, she concludes that these laws amount to a concerted attempt to discourage certain groups from participating in democracy.

Anderson's writing, while meticulously researched, has a partisan tone in the sense that the voter suppression strategies she describes are almost all concocted by Republican operatives to reduce Democratic votes. Yet whether or not they agree with her politics, Christians in particular ought to grapple with her book. After all, as Martin Luther King Jr. taught us, securing equal rights for all citizens is fundamentally a moral cause, not a political one: it reflects the truth that each person is created equally in the image of God.

Maid: Hard Work, Low Pay, and a Mother's Will to Survive
Stephanie Land
(Hachette)

A much-anticipated January debut, *Maid* is being compared to Barbara Ehrenreich's muckraking *Nickel and Dimed* for the way it sheds light on the appalling conditions of those who clean the homes of the rich. But Land's memoir is, if anything, even more dispiriting. This is no journalist going undercover with an easy ticket out at any time, but a young woman and her daughter trapped in debasing poverty and a maze of inadequate social services, with little prospect of ever escaping. (Land finds her way out, and a book deal, though she cautions against viewing her success as exemplary; most women like her, no matter how much pluck and grit they muster, will never get a chance to tell their tale.)

As a housecleaner, Land sees the dirty underside of affluent lives, and doesn't envy their vacuous success in the least. So (whether by design or not) her book ends up being more than a simplistic indictment of a wealthy society that fails its poor; many of the problems she describes are beyond the scope of any government fix. Her own story is a case in point. Land is plunged into poverty in the first place after escaping domestic abuse, having cohabited and conceived a child with a man who didn't want one.

Land's book gives sharp insights into the lives of today's working poor and offers ample reason for all people of good will to take up their cause. It also, unintentionally, suggests an additional response. Land (and the thousands like her) needs a living wage, affordable housing, and decent schools. But just as much, she – no less than the rich-but-unsatisfied denizens of the homes she cleans – could use a community: one that's ready to come alongside her and her daughter to provide friendship, advice, and practical and spiritual support. ⇘ *The Editors*

REVIEW

SALLY THOMAS

Litanies of Reclamation

A review of The Lost Words: A Spell Book
by Robert Macfarlane and Jackie Morris

Jackie Morris,
Kingfishers,
from *The Lost
Words*

For everything you bring into your house,
take something out. Who hasn't encountered, by now, some version of this useful
de-cluttering principle? But imagine applying
it to more than clothes and knickknacks.
Imagine it as a rule for language, so that every
time you added a word to your vocabulary –

selfie, say, or *subtweet* – you had to remove an
older word to make room for it.

The Lost Words, a stunning new poetry
picture book by Robert Macfarlane and Jackie
Morris, responds to this very situation. In the
latest edition of the *Oxford Junior Dictionary,*
a standard primary-school reference text, new

Sally Thomas is the author of two poetry chapbooks, Fallen Water *(2015) and* Richeldis of
Walsingham *(2016). Her poetry and fiction have appeared recently or are forthcoming in* Barren
Magazine, Mezzo Cammin, North Carolina Literary Review, The Orchards Poetry Journal, Wild
Goose Poetry Review, *and* The Windhover. *She lives with her family in North Carolina.*

Plough Quarterly • *Winter 2019*

coinages like *blog* and *voicemail* have forced the exclusion – no doubt because paper costs money, and school dictionaries shouldn't weigh more than the children who use them – of a whole body of words that evoke the natural world.

Presumably the dictionary is designed to reflect current usage among children, and presumably today's children are talking more about the internet than they are about the woods. But I wonder which comes first: the actual extinction of words, or their removal from view, so that people who might have used them, or at least wondered about them, don't? Perhaps the chicken-egg answer doesn't matter nearly as much as what we stand to lose. If we lack the language to name for ourselves the realities that surround us, what does that do to our perception of them?

The fading of nature words – *acorn, bluebell, dandelion, heron, otter, wren* – from the active language of children strikes me as a kind of poverty. Too often, of course, this poverty intersects with material poverty. An art-teacher friend once described for me a class she taught in an inner-city public high school, in the course of which she was trying to explain what *texture* meant. "Like bark," she told them. They looked at her. "You know," she said. "The bark on a tree? Its skin?" Thirty pairs of teenaged eyes returned to her the flat gaze of total incomprehension. Trees had skin? Who knew? Who cared?

"Well, what was I going to do?" she said to me later. "I made them get up out of those chairs, moaning and groaning, and we went outside, and we spent the rest of the hour touching trees." Note, by the way, that there *were* trees in those students' immediate environment. Some urban landscapes are, I know, concrete deserts, but in even the lowest-income neighborhoods in this particular

Southern city where my friend and I then lived, trees grow thickly, profusely, lushly, but apparently – to children who have never been called on to notice them – invisibly.

As far as my friend's students were concerned, *bark* was what dogs did, and that was that. Lacking language, they lacked access to real and imaginative territory in their own world. This lack may be attributed, with some plausibility, to other lacks they experienced. But it is a lack not limited to situations of economic deprivation. Any child, anywhere, at any socio-economic level, may be vulnerable to the same poverty, the same blindness. All it takes is for some crucial adult in that child's life to consider that dandelions, for example, are not worth the bother of naming.

In *The Lost Words*, Macfarlane and Morris aim to restore an imaginative vision of the natural world. Macfarlane might have contented himself with simply listing and defining those words lost to the dictionary, pairing them with Morris's breathtaking illustrations. An illustrated nature dictionary would have been, in itself, a magical-enough book. But in making each "lost word" a poem, Macfarlane has revived not only the word itself, but language as an experience. The book's subtitle labels it "A Spell Book," and its poems are incantatory, each one a litany of reclamation.

As the American poet Dana Gioia has put it, this is *poetry as enchantment*. What does that mean? In his essay of that title, Gioia notes Robert Frost's definition of poetry as a means of remembering, "which is to say a mnemonic technology to preserve human experience." Frost, himself a dedicated chronicler of the natural world, maintained,

> ## *Which comes first: the actual extinction of words, or their removal from view?*

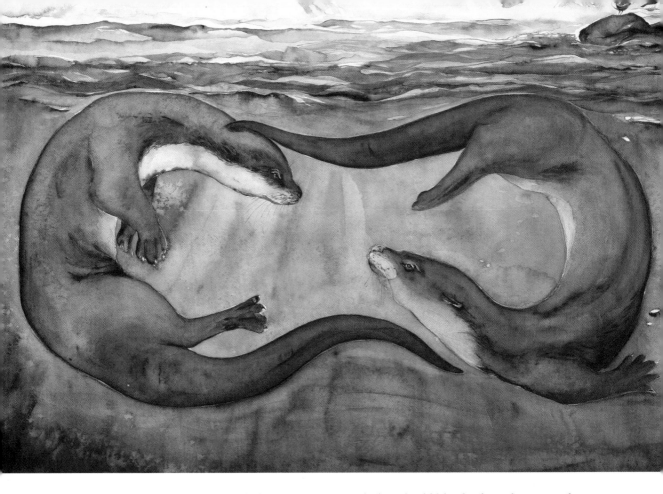

Jackie Morris,
Otters, from
*The Lost
Words*

as Gioia says, that the loss of what it preserves "would impoverish us." This is to say that poetry enriches human consciousness or, at the very least, protects things of common value from depredation. Finally, he asserts that poetry guards against the human danger "to forget." Here Frost acknowledges that the art opposes the natural forces of time, mortality, and oblivion, which humanity must face to discover and preserve its meaning. As Frost said elsewhere, one of the essential tasks of poetry is to give us "a clarification of life . . . a momentary stay against confusion."

Many of us may feel as numb to the declarative power of poetry as we are to the textured reality of nature. For instance, we might have had Frost's "Stopping by Woods on a Snowy Evening" explicated to us by our eleventh-grade English teacher as a poem about suicidal ideation, full stop, because the woods are dark and cold like death, and snow is white, which is a color symbolically associated with death. If this has been our experience, then it's understandable that we might struggle to see the forest for the death wish. Meanwhile, the poem's undeniable music – ". . . the sweep / Of easy wind and downy flake" – goes unheard. It is precisely this music that generates the "mnemonic technology" Dana Gioia describes. While it might be entertaining to speculate about the poem's darker meanings, the memorable *experience* of it is far more immediate and physical than any abstruse speculations. Its patterns of meter and rhyme make it an easy poem to memorize, a deeply pleasurable poem to recite aloud. And if we should find ourselves in the woods on a snowy night, then we have something to say about that: "the woods are lovely, dark, and deep." In saying it, letting the alliteration roll off the tongue, we know something. We see it. It exists for us.

This same "mnemonic technology" is at work in *The Lost Words*. The poems in this book are acrostics: each letter of a "lost word" begins a poetic line. The effect is one of opening-out, the word expanding to contain an entire linguistic ecosystem. Take, for example, the first two lines of "otter:"

> **O**tter enters river without falter – what a
> supple slider out of holt and into water!
> **T**his shape-shifter's a sheer breath-taker, a
> sure heart-stopper – but you'll only ever
> spot a shadow-flutter, bubble-skein, and
> never (almost never) actual otter.

In this poem, each line moves from internal rhyme to internal rhyme. In the first line, the feminine rhymes of *otter, falter, water,* plus the additional, masculine-rhymed *river* and *slider,* establish a pattern that suffuses the whole poem with forward movement. The reading ear alerts itself continually to the next instance of rhyme, slipping forward through the lines even as the otter slips down the bank and into the water. Too, in its persistent alliteration and its repetition of hyphenated names – *shape-shifter, breath-taker, heart-stopper, shadow-flutter, bubble-skein, silver-miner, inside-outer* – the poem echoes the Anglo-Saxon poetic line, held together by its emphatic consonants and illuminated by its kennings. This resonance suggests another recovery from extinction by amnesia, that of the English poetic tradition itself. Meanwhile, where the lines run on, visually, as if they were prose, these devices sustain the necessary tension and density that mark what looks like a paragraph as not a paragraph, but a line of poetry, in simultaneous conversation with its subject and its tradition.

Similar phenomena occur throughout the book. "Here hunts heron. Here haunts heron," begins the poem about that leggy water bird,

its alliterative stresses hammered home. But note the sleight-of-hand that also occurs in this line. Slip in one letter, and *hunt* becomes *haunt*. Nature opens into the supernatural: bird becomes spirit, though the next line transfigures him again into something mechanical: the "huge-hinged heron." Again and again, the poems enact these incantations. In an instance of levity, they conjure the newt:

> "Newt, oh newt, you are too cute!"
> Emoted the coot to the too-cute newt
> "With your frilly back and your shiny suit and
> your spotted skin so unhirsute!"

The newt poem calls up the rhyme-patterns of rap, with its constant and surprising experimentations in sound. And the fern poem summons the ghost of Robert Frost. Its trimeter opening line, "Fern's first frond is furled," echoes Frost's "Nature's first green is gold," even in the palimpsest of an end-rhyme. If these are poems about natural history, they are also poems about the natural history of poetry itself. They invite the reader to a sharpened vision of the natural world, but they also extend an invitation to savor the English language as its own fascinating and accessible ecosystem.

I marvel at this book for its own virtues, but I also marvel that a book like this was created *for children*. We too often underestimate children, at least if our television programming for them is any indication. Even those earnest public-television children's shows on whose ancestors I grew up, and which my own children watched, subscribe heavily to the theme of *Reading Is Good, and If You Watch This Half-Hour Program, You'll Know Why.* Meanwhile, many children's books seem to

We too often underestimate children, at least if our television programming for them is any indication.

Jackie Morris,
Dandelion,
from *The Lost
Words*

assume that children occupy some lower rung of the evolutionary ladder where the apogee of cultural expression is the fart joke.

While I can think of beautiful, poetic, nature-themed picture books for children – Jane Yolen's *Owl Moon*, for example – it is harder to call to mind books of poetry for children that show the same intelligence and attention to craft which their authors bring to bear in their work for adults. In this slender category I would include Richard Wilbur's hilarious *Opposites*, and the children's poems of the Cornish poet Charles Causley, between whose writing for adults and whose writing for children the line is very fine indeed. Like Causley, who could write a comic poem beginning, "The Reverend Rundle, his gear in a bundle," and then shift in an instant to the hauntingly elegiac – "'Love

is not here,' the hawthorn said" – Macfarlane presumes the child's capacity for a whole range of human emotion, all predicated on wonder, as well as the child's ability to follow and thrill to the complex play of the English language.

The child who reads this book may, I hope, become an adult who still marvels at the crushed sunlit scent of a dandelion. More than that, I think it's reasonable to hope that the same child, grown to adulthood, might experience poetry, too – not as alien, uninviting, or simply beneath notice, but as a world in which he or she is instinctively at home and alive. In what might be called our post-enchantment age, it is remarkable to encounter a book that offers, without irony and with high seriousness, the dual enchantments of nature and poetry. ⤙

The Children of Pyongyang

STEPHEN YOON

Stephen Yoon is a Korean American doctor who for the last decade has cared for children with disabilities in Pyongyang, North Korea. Until last year, he lived there with his wife, Joy, and their three children as members of IGNIS Community. US government restrictions have now made it impossible for the family to return to Pyongyang.

Children at a kindergarten in North Korea

Plough: *What first inspired you to move to North Korea?*

Stephen Yoon: In 2006, I attended a church meeting where a man spoke about his service work in North Korea. He had witnessed the aftermath of the famine of 1994, which had claimed the lives of three million people. Though relief supplies arrived from around the world, this man asked himself, "Would Jesus send food to North Korea, or would he actually go there?" He felt that Jesus would go to be with people and share their suffering and show them love.

I was inspired and later shared his story with my wife. We were living an ordinary life in California at the time. Joy said, "Let's pack up and go!"

So you went . . .

Yes. In 2007, we moved to Rajin province, an experimental free-trade zone that borders China and Russia. I worked in a clinic. Since North Korea is a socialist country, almost every aspect of life is related to the government. We interacted with government officials within our designated departments on a daily basis.

Therapy for a child with cerebral palsy

Korea, we were shocked to see all the different people living together, and all the problems they brought with them. Seeing how these problems could be solved gave us hope and formed the model for our developing ministry, named IGNIS Community.

Our current community includes over forty people working on a variety of projects in North Korea. Some are full members; others come for one-year or six-month internships, helping with projects. There are members from many nations. Some are health care workers, some are kindergarten staff, some are aid workers.

We made it clear to the North Korean government that we were coming as Christians to help North Korea, and this was permitted and acknowledged. Still, we are not permitted to distribute religious material or speak about our faith.

A few years ago, within a relatively brief period, several of my coworkers experienced life-threatening events. Then Joy was diagnosed with kidney cancer and returned to the United States after major surgery. Thankfully, she recovered, but I was shaken. Until then I'd been very focused on my work, but I finally realized that work is not the most important thing.

I looked at John 16: "If you love one another, the world will know that you are my disciples." Learning how to live together in love and care for one another like brothers and sisters became central to my life. Now I see this – and not work – as my main calling.

What were some of your day-to-day challenges?

As foreigners and US citizens we faced more restrictions over what we were allowed to do without a government escort. Arranging our schedule was challenging since IGNIS Community's eight-member team in Pyong-yang shared one vehicle and one official who was responsible for the work schedule. Our team also lived together in one house because of the lack of housing for foreigners. These dynamics can be challenging.

Despite the restrictions, we were amazed by what we had freedom to do. Our daily work involved interacting with regular people in a local hospital. We treated patients and educated doctors. As long as we allowed enough time to receive the proper permission, we found there was little we could not do.

How did your community in North Korea form?

When Joy and I visited Jesus Abbey, a community in the mountains of northeastern South

How does your faith inform your vocation?

As a student in South Korea, I was poor at math. I felt called to serve in medicine, but becoming a doctor seemed impossible. Still, I thought, "God makes impossible things possible." I knew what I was called to do, and I was given the faith that it could happen. One of my patients in Rajin was unable to

move her hands. I laid my hands on her, and, amazingly, she got better. After that, "incurable" patients began flocking to the clinic. This experience made me realize I should not rely upon my own strength but on God's power.

How did you become involved with patients with cerebral palsy and autism spectrum disorder?

News of my work in Rajin spread to Pyongyang, and the medical school contacted me. They told me that if I got a degree from Kim Il Sung University, my work would be better accepted. So in 2011, I became the first foreigner to receive a doctorate in rehabilitation from Pyongyang Medical School.

Then in January 2012, I met a five-year-old with cerebral palsy in Rajin. Bok Shin was paraplegic and could not swallow, so her grandmother chewed food for her and put it in her mouth. I tried to take care of Bok Shin with love. Soon she began to move her fingers.

That same year, Pyongyang Medical School invited me to teach, but I was worried Bok Shin would die if I left. I asked if she could be moved from Rajin to Pyongyang Children's Hospital. The head of the hospital was surprised when I told him what Bok Shin's condition was. He said there were no patients with cerebral palsy in North Korea. I just asked for Bok Shin to be given a bed, which she received.

When I began taking care of Bok Shin in Pyongyang, the parents of other patients remembered children in their neighborhoods with similar symptoms. Word spread. From all over North Korea, parents brought their children with disabilities to Pyongyang. The hospital staff didn't know what to do with all of them. I began providing therapy there, in collaboration with the medical school.

That October, I started working with another paraplegic child, Oo-Ein. When I asked her what she wished for most, she said, "To walk to school with my friends." Her teacher had been carrying her to school on her back. After a year of intense therapy, Oo-Ein walked out of the hospital. I said to her, "What is your dream now?"

She answered, "To become a doctor like you when I grow up, so that I can help kids like me." The hospital staff was moved to tears.

The government reacted very favorably to this story, and Chairman Kim Jong-Un decided that doctors should be educated to treat people with disabilities and sent across North Korea to

Stephen Yoon coaches doctors in the Pyongyang Medical School Hospital.

treat children. So I began working with Pyong-yang Medical School to develop a curriculum to teach North Korean doctors how to treat cerebral palsy and autism. Three doctors have been trained and sent to other hospitals, and I trained four recent residents in pediatric rehabilitation.

After we received permission to train doctors in pediatric rehab, we were introduced to an American physical therapist who began visiting North Korea and treating children with autism. Before June 2015, there was no diagnosis or therapy of any kind available for children with Autism Spectrum Disorder in North Korea. Children with ASD and their parents struggled to cope with the challenges that faced them. Now over thirty doctors from Pyongyang Medical School Hospital, Pyongyang Children's Hospital, and the DPRK Disability Federation have taken part in a lecture series on autism, and families with children who have autism are receiving treatment for the first time.

What has changed over this past year for your ministry as the Geographic Travel Restriction has been put into place?

In July 2017 the US State Department issued a Geographic Travel Restriction (GTR) for North Korea, which has greatly impacted both our family and our work. This change came in direct response to Otto Warmbier's detainment and death.

However, Otto's situation is the exception to life as a foreigner in North Korea. Approximately two hundred US citizens have been working and living in North Korea over the past few decades. Throughout these years only a handful have been detained.

Now, due to political tensions, our personal family situation, although not tragic, is disappointing. We have been traveling from country to country since the beginning of September 2018 because we do not have residence visas for any Asian country besides North Korea, and we do not currently have a home in the United States.

Our desire is to return to Pyongyang as a family. Unfortunately, the US State Department has granted only adults on our project Special Validation Passports to travel to North Korea. They have informed us that minors will not be issued special passports to travel to North Korea.

Our children are grieved by this situation. We have invested many years in our work and life in North Korea. It is a shame to lose all that we have worked so hard for. Until the travel ban is lifted we will be unable to return to full-time work in North Korea.

What is the future focus for IGNIS Community?

The direction of IGNIS Community has not changed. We remain undeterred to share love with the people of North Korea. It is our calling to live among the people, demonstrate our love for them by building relationships with them, and develop sustainable solutions to social needs.

Since US citizens are now only able to enter North Korea on an extremely limited basis, our American team members are focused on developing leaders from other countries and supporting, from outside North Korea, the work that continues on the inside.

What advice do you have for those who want to help people in North Korea?

We believe that meaningful engagement in North Korea makes a positive difference. Our medical, humanitarian, and development work not only helps the most vulnerable of its society and changes people's perspectives on life, but also bridges the gap between our countries.

Prayer and advocacy are needed to bring peace to the Korean Peninsula. Please join us in praying for peace between the United States and North Korea. Our work is incredibly

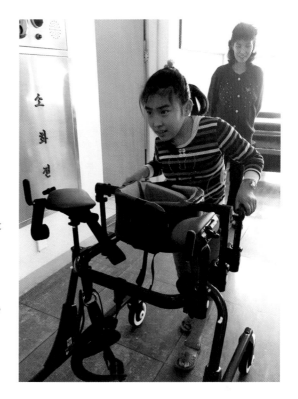

complex as we now have to deal with US and UN sanctions, the GTR, and the visa complexities for traveling in all countries involved.

Please pray for foreign Christians living and working inside North Korea. It is not easy living in an isolated and constrained environment, so we often feel overwhelmed and discouraged. Pray that we will have the endurance and fortitude to follow through with our calling.

Finally, please pray for the treatment and acceptance of children with disabilities in North Korea. We are dedicated to establishing the first-ever treatment center for children with cerebral palsy and autism, but our work is far from done. ⤳

This interview was conducted by Sung Hoon Park in April 2016 and October 2018. Joy's book, Discovering Joy: Ten Years in North Korea *(Klug, 2018), details her family's experiences.* joyinnorthkorea.com. *To learn more about IGNIS Community visit* igniscommunity.org.

A child learns how to walk using a gait trainer donated by the Bruderhof, the community behind *Plough.*

Cancilde and Emmanuel

How far does forgiveness reach?

DENISE UWIMANA

Denise Uwimana lost her husband in the Rwandan genocide of 1994. She and her three young sons survived, thanks in part to Hutu neighbors who sheltered them. In April, to mark the twenty-fifth anniversary of that event, Plough *will publish her book* From Red Earth: A Rwandan Story of Healing and Forgiveness, *from which this story is taken.*

Above: The author, Cancilde, and Emmanuel

I N 2015 I RETURNED to Mukoma, my murdered husband's village, for the yearly remembrance of all who died in the genocide against the Tutsi. I knew the village would expect to hear from me, and now I suddenly felt that this was the time and place – twenty-one years after the genocide, in an atmosphere of peace – to broach the subject of forgiveness.

Despite my certainty, I felt apprehensive as I rose to address around five hundred people. Were they ready for this? "Has any of you been able to forgive?" I asked. To my astonishment, at least a dozen hands shot up, voices calling, "I have!" "I have!"

One was Cancilde. I knew that her husband and five of her seven children had been killed; one son and daughter had survived, having been absent on the fatal day. All eyes were on this bereaved mother as she stood to speak. "A gang of Interahamwe mobbed my house on April 9, 1994," she began, referring to the Hutu militias that led the genocide. "My family was caught by surprise."

She stalled, then plunged on. "A young neighbor, Emmanuel, killed my husband and five of our children. He was arrested and imprisoned the next year. But three years ago, in 2012, he was released. Before going home, Emmanuel tried to come to my house, to humble himself. But the village had learned of his arrival and staged a protest, so he could not come that night. Next morning, however, he appeared at my door, pleading for forgiveness. 'From that day to this,' he told me, 'I have felt continual shame.'"

Cancilde paused again, then concluded quietly, "My heart had been freed from hate by then, because we widows had been reading the gospel together. Its message prepared my heart to forgive."

FOUR MONTHS LATER, on my next visit to Mukoma, Cancilde came to greet me. A reticent man walked at her side. "Welcome back, Denise," Cancilde said. "I want you to meet Emmanuel."

A teenager in 1994, Emmanuel had heard the radio's repeated instructions to annihilate all Tutsi, had smelled the smoke of distant fires, had sensed the brewing excitement. When Interahamwe burst into Mukoma in their banana-leaf headgear, he was ready for their summons. Their exhilarating extermination song, *Tuza batsembe tsembe*, thrilled him. This was better than the frenzy of football fans, he thought – this time he'd be part of the action.

"Anyone who doesn't kill is not a man!" the leader incited his followers. "It's time to get to work. Eradicate all snakes! And remember, young vipers are as deadly as full-grown ones."

With that, they surged forward, still singing their rousing song. Emmanuel grabbed a machete to join the charge. Then, zealous to prove his manhood, he attacked Cancilde's home.

When Emmanuel was arrested the following year, a new government had replaced the old, and murder was no longer the order of the day. It was in prison that reality struck. As he tried to subsist in the filthy, crowded conditions, year after year, Emmanuel was haunted by the faces of the children he had killed.

He was aghast at what he had done. What had possessed him to commit such unspeakable deeds? The mental torture was so intense, he was certain hell could be no worse. In July 2000, Emmanuel confessed his crimes and tried to express the guilt engulfing him.

THERE WAS NO WAY the judicial system could process nearly 130,000 charges of participation in genocide, especially since most judges and lawyers were dead or had fled. So in 2002, the new government instituted gacaca – pronounced "gachacha" – throughout the country. These tribunals were based on the traditional system of dealing justice, using trusted men and women in each locale as judges or *inyangamugayo*, "those who hate dishonesty."

From Red Earth
A Rwandan Story of Healing and Forgiveness
Denise Uwimana
April 2019 • Softcover • 220 pages • Plough

If this were only a memoir of a genocide survivor's long, hard road to personal healing, it would be remarkable enough. But Denise Uwimana didn't stop there. Leaving a secure job in business, she devoted the rest of her life to restoring her country by empowering other genocide widows to band together, tell their stories, find healing, and rebuild their lives. The stories she has uncovered through her work and recounted here illustrate the complex and unfinished work of truth-telling, recovery, and reconciliation that may be Rwanda's lasting legacy.

Get the book at *plough.com/fromredearth*.

A cluster of villages would gather weekly, at some central outdoor location, until all cases from their area had been heard. Anyone present could question the accused, who were transported from prison. *Inyangamugayo* considered statements from both sides before handing down a verdict. They had authority to grant reduced sentences if the accused admitted guilt and showed remorse. Some convicts were assigned daytime work release, to help rebuild the nation.

These trials were traumatic for the whole country. For survivors, hearing details of their loved ones' murders, after so many years, tore open scabbing wounds. Killers, in their pink prison uniforms, felt humiliated at having their acts publicly exposed. Their families, too, felt shamed.

But for some, both victims and perpetrators, this excruciating process was a step toward healing. Gacaca confessions helped many survivors locate their relatives' remains, so they could honor them in burial. And for contrite killers, humbling themselves brought a measure of relief.

In 2003, Cancilde was terrified at the thought of facing her family's murderer, but gacaca attendance was mandatory. Also, despite her anxiety, she needed to know the truth of how her husband and children had died. So she forced herself to walk to the designated gathering place beneath large shade trees.

When it was Emmanuel's turn to speak, he stood and faced the populace, but his eyes were cast down. Struggling to describe the worst deed of his life, he told how he and five other militants had descended on Cancilde's house the first day of Mukoma's atrocities.

"The five others prevented the family from escaping, and they goaded me on – but it is I, Emmanuel, who committed the murders," he stated. Emmanuel was sweating and trembling as he recounted the details. "I was rewarded for killing this family," he added. "In payment, Interahamwe gave me Cancilde's house. I took it apart and used the materials to build myself a home, where I lived till I was arrested in 1995."

Lifting his eyes to look wildly around at the set, stony faces, Emmanuel cried, "I plead for mercy from the government, from my village, and from God!"

Cancilde was shaking with sobs at the report she had just heard. Yet Emmanuel's honesty and anguish reached through her pain and touched her heart. The picture of his contorted face remained etched in her mind.

Gacaca judges sentenced the young man to twenty-five years in prison for his crimes. Because of his remorse, however, he was released after seventeen. That's when he appeared at Cancilde's door.

When the lonely mother opened to his knock, she saw the killer of her husband and children standing before her. His eyes filled with tears, Emmanuel repeated his heartfelt plea.

"Yes, I forgive you," she had said.

NOW HERE I WAS, in August 2015, standing in the road with both of them. Emmanuel had been looking at the ground; now his eyes met mine.

"Cancilde has become like a mother to me," he said quietly. "When I need advice, I go to her. Before I got married, I talked over the details with her. She is the local official who authorized my marriage."

Cancilde broke in, "Emmanuel is the one I ask for help when my house needs repair. He comes any time I ask, to replace a window or mend the roof. If my cow has problems, I call him. And he knows he's always welcome to share a meal at my home. He is my son!"

They looked at each other, and Emmanuel smiled shyly. ➤

The Blessed Woman of Nazareth

ALFRED DELP

Mary is the most comforting of all the Advent figures. Advent's holiest consolation is that the angel's annunciation met with a ready heart in Mary. The Word became flesh, and in the holy place of a motherly heart the earth gave birth to a world of God-humanity. What good does it do us to sense and feel our misery unless a bridge is thrown over to the other shore? What help is it to be terrified at our lostness and confusion unless a light flashes up that is a match for darkness and always is its master? What good does it do us to shiver in the coldness and hardness in which the world freezes as it goes deeper astray in itself and kills itself, unless we also come to know of the grace that is mightier than the peril of oblivion?

Gérard David, *The Annunciation* (detail)

Alfred Delp (1907–1945) was a German Jesuit priest who was condemned to die for his open opposition to the Nazi regime. This meditation, which he wrote while in prison, appears in When the Time Was Fulfilled: Christmas Meditations *(Plough, 1967). Get the free ebook at* plough.com/timefulfilled.

Gérard David, *The Annunciation*

Poets and myth-makers and other tellers of stories and fairy tales have often spoken of mothers. Sometimes they meant the earth; other times, nature. By this word they tried to disclose the mysterious creative fount of all things, to conjure up the welling mystery of life. In all this there was hunger and anticipation and longing and Advent-waiting for this blessed woman.

That God became a mother's son; that there could be a woman walking the earth whose womb was consecrated to be the holy temple and tabernacle of God – that is actually earth's perfection and the fulfillment of its expectations.

So many kinds of Advent consolation stream from the mysterious figure of the blessed, expectant Mary. The grey horizons must grow light. It is only the immediate

Raphael, *The Sistine Madonna* (detail)

scene that shouts so loudly and insistently. Beyond the present tumult there exists a different realm, one that is now in our midst. The woman has conceived the Child, sheltered him beneath her heart, and given birth to the Son. The world has come under a different law. Christmas is not only a historic event that happened once, on which our salvation rests. Christmas is the promise of a new order of things, of life, of our existence.

We must remember that the blessed woman of Nazareth, like John the Baptist and the angel of annunciation, is an illuminating figure of life, of our existence. Deep down in her being, our days and our destinies bear the blessing and mystery of God. The blessed woman waits, and we must wait too until her hour has come. We must be patient and wait with readiness for the moment when it pleases the Lord to appear anew in our night too. ⇒

Christoph Wetzel, *Untitled,* charcoal, 2008

New Heaven, New War

ROBERT SOUTHWELL

This little babe, so few days old,
Is come to rifle Satan's fold;
All hell doth at his presence quake.
Though he himself for cold do shake,
For in this weak unarmèd wise
The gates of hell he will surprise.

With tears he fights and wins the field;
His naked breast stands for a shield;
His battering shot are babish cries,
His arrows looks of weeping eyes,
His martial ensigns cold and need,
And feeble flesh his warrior's steed.

His camp is pitchèd in a stall,
His bulwark but a broken wall,
The crib his trench, hay stalks his stakes,
Of shepherds he his muster makes;
And thus, as sure his foe to wound,
The angels' trumps alarum sound.

My soul, with Christ join thou in fight;
Stick to the tents that he hath pight;
Within his crib is surest ward,
This little babe will be thy guard.
If thou wilt foil thy foes with joy,
Then flit not from this heavenly boy.

Robert Southwell (ca. 1561–1595), a Jesuit priest, was a poet and underground Catholic missionary to his native England. Arrested as a traitor, he endured three years of imprisonment, including torture, before his execution. He was canonized as a martyr in 1970 by Pope Paul VI.

Albrecht Dürer, *Angel with a Lute*, 1497

Born to Us

MARTIN LUTHER

The angel said to them, "Behold, I bring you good tidings of great joy which shall be to all the people; for there is born to you this day a Savior, who is Christ the Lord." Luke 2:10

THE GOSPEL teaches that Christ was born, and that he died and suffered everything on our behalf, as is here declared by the angel. In these words you clearly see that he is born for us.

He does not simply say, Christ is born, but to *you* he is born, neither does he say, I bring glad tidings, but to *you* I bring glad tidings of great joy. Furthermore, this joy was not to remain in Christ, but it shall be to all the people. . . . For this purpose Christ willed to be born, that through him we might be born anew.

Martin Luther (1483–1546) was an outlaw monk taking refuge in Wartburg Castle when he delivered the 1521 Christmas sermon from which this reading is taken.

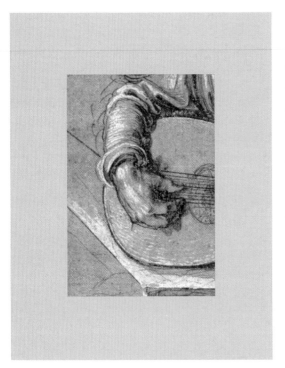

Christ be born in you. This will be the case if you believe, then you will repose in the lap of the Virgin Mary and be her dear child. But you must exercise this faith and pray while you live; you cannot establish it too firmly. This is our foundation and inheritance, upon which good works must be built.

THE GOSPEL does not merely teach about the history of Christ. No, it enables all who believe it to receive it as their own, which is the way the Gospel operates. Of what benefit would it be to me if Christ had been born a thousand times, and it would daily be sung into my ears in a most lovely manner, if I were never to hear that he was born for me and was to be my very own? If the voice gives forth this pleasant sound, even if it be in homely phrase, my heart listens with joy for it is a lovely sound which penetrates the soul. If now there were anything else to be preached, the evangelical angel and the angelic evangelist would certainly have touched upon it.

If Christ has indeed become your own, and you have by such faith been cleansed through him and have received your inheritance without any personal merit, it follows that you will do good works by doing to your neighbor as Christ has done to you. Here good works are their own teacher. What are the good works of Christ? Is it not true that they are good because they have been done for your benefit, for God's sake, who commanded him to do the works in your behalf? In this then Christ was obedient to the Father, in that he loved and served us.

Therefore since you have received enough and become rich, you have no other commandment than to serve Christ and render obedience to him. Direct your works that they may be of benefit to your neighbor, just as the

Christ helps us so we in return help our neighbor, and all have enough.

O, this is the great joy of which the angel speaks. This is the comfort and exceeding goodness of God that, if anyone believes this, he can boast of the treasure that Mary is his rightful mother, Christ his brother, and God his father. For these things actually occurred and are true, but we must believe. This is the principal thing and the principal treasure in every Gospel. Christ must above all things become our own and we become his. This is what is meant by Isaiah: "Unto us a child is born, unto us a son is given." To us, to us, to us is born, and to us is given this child.

Therefore see to it that you do not treat the Gospel only as history, for that is only transient; neither regard it only as an example, for it is of no value without faith. Rather, see to it that you make this birth your own and that works of Christ are of benefit to you. For this reason Jesus said at the Last Supper: "This is my commandment that you love one another; even as I have loved you." Here it is seen that he loved us and did everything for our benefit, in order that we may do the same, not to him, for he needs it not, but to our neighbor. This is his commandment, and this is our obedience. Christ helps us so we in return help our neighbor, and all have enough.

NOTICE, THEN, how far off those are who expend their energies uniting good works with stone. Of what benefit is it to your neighbor if you build a church entirely out of gold? Of what benefit to him is the frequent ringing of great church bells? Of what benefit to him is the glitter and the ceremonies in the churches, the priests' gowns, the sanctuary, the silver pictures and vessels? Of what benefit to him are the many candles and much incense? Of what benefit to him is the much chanting and mumbling, the singing of vigils and masses? Do you think that God wants to be served with the sound of bells, the smoke of candles, the glitter of gold and such fancies? He has commanded none of these, but if you see your neighbor going astray, sinning, or suffering in body or soul, you are to leave everything else and at once help him in every way in your power and if you can do no more, help him with words of comfort and prayer. Thus has Christ done to you and given you an example to follow.

Here Jesus does what he says, "And the poor have good tidings preached to them," and "Blessed are the poor in spirit; for theirs is the kingdom of heaven" (Matt. 11:5; 5:3). Here are no learned, no rich, no mighty ones, for such people do not as a rule accept the Gospel.

The Gospel is a heavenly treasure, which will not tolerate any other treasure, and will not agree with any earthly guest in the heart. Therefore whoever loves the one must let go the other, as Christ says, "You cannot serve God and mammon" (Matt. 6:24).

This is shown by the shepherds in that they were in the field, under the canopy of heaven, and not in houses, showing that they do not hold fast and cling to temporal things. And besides being in the fields by night, they are despised by and unknown to the world which sleeps in the night, and by day delights so to walk that it may be noticed; but the poor shepherds go about their work at night. They represent all the lowly who live on earth, often despised and unnoticed, who dwell only under the protection of heaven; they eagerly desire the Gospel.

The Gospel is a heavenly treasure, which will not tolerate any other treasure.

works are nothing and are condemned before God, for it does not easily give up its prejudices and presumptions.

THEREFORE let us beware of all teaching that does not set forth Christ. What more would you know? What more do you need, if indeed you know Christ, as above set forth, if you walk by faith in God, and by love to your neighbor, doing to them as Christ has done to you? This is indeed the whole Scripture in its briefest form, that no more words or books are necessary, but only life and action.

Let everyone examine himself in the light of the Gospel and see how far he is from Christ, what is the character of his faith and love. There are many who are enkindled with dreamy devotion, and when they hear of such poverty of Christ, they are almost angry with the citizens of Bethlehem. They denounce their blindness and ingratitude, and think that if they had been there, they would have shown the Lord and his mother a more kindly service, and would not have permitted them to be treated so miserably. But they do not look by their side to see how many of their fellow humans need their help, and which they ignore in their misery. Who is there upon earth that has no poor, miserable, sick, erring ones around him? Why does he not exercise his love to those? Why does he not do to them as Christ has done to him?

No more words or books are necessary, but only life and action.

That there were shepherds means that no one is to hear the Gospel for himself alone, but everyone is to tell it to others who are not acquainted with it. For he who believes for himself has enough and should endeavor to bring others to such faith and knowledge, so that one may be a shepherd of the other, to wait upon and lead him into the pasture of the Gospel in this world, during the nighttime of this earthly life. At first the shepherds were sore afraid because of the angel; for human nature is shocked when it first hears in the Gospel that all our

Source: "Sermon for Christmas Day; Luke 2:1–14" in *The Sermons of Martin Luther* (Lutherans in All Lands Press, 1906).

This is one of forty-five selections in the Plough *anthology* Watch for the Light: Readings for Advent and Christmas, *which includes authors such as Aquinas, Bonhoeffer, Day, and Gutiérrez.*

A Trio of Lenten Readers

MAUREEN SWINGER

THE FIRST WEEKS after New Year are a prelude to the holiest time of the Christian calendar – Lent, Passion Week, and Easter. In preparing for this season each year, we on the *Plough* staff find ourselves turning repeatedly to a handful of proven spiritual classics. Among them are three devotional volumes from *Plough*'s own backlist. These titles may be familiar to some readers, but for others will (we hope) come as a welcome discovery.

Johann Ernst von Holst's *The Crucified Is My Love* is a small treasure from 1895, first published in English in 2017. The author, a Lutheran pastor from the Baltic town of Wenden (now Cēsis, Latvia), wrote these morning and evening Lenten meditations for his German-speaking congregation. Each short reading builds a vivid, detailed account around a central Gospel verse.

Valued for the single-hearted love it expresses for the suffering Christ, von Holst's book was passed down by his parishioners to their descendants through four generations. Eighty-five years after it was written, a copy came into the hands of a *Plough* editor, Kathleen Hasenberg, whom we have to thank for her sensitive translation.

Bread and Wine: Readings for Lent and Easter comes in a sturdy hardcover that can withstand forty-six days of lying open around the house. There are readings for each day from Ash Wednesday to Holy Saturday, grouped into four sections: "Invitation," "Temptation," "Passion," and "Crucifixion." For Easter itself and the weeks following it, twenty-six additional readings take the reader on into the victory of the risen Christ.

The book's spirit is summed up in the introduction: "Lent is meant to be the church's springtime, a time when, out of the darkness of sin's winter, a repentant, empowered people emerges. No wonder one liturgy refers to it as 'this joyful season.'"

Bread and Wine features selections from beloved spiritual writers ancient and modern – including Saint Augustine, Thomas à Kempis, G. K. Chesterton, Dietrich Bonhoeffer, Fleming Rutledge, and N. T. Wright – as well as poetry by John Donne, Christina Rossetti, John Updike, Geoffrey Hill, and others.

The final title, *Easter Stories: Classic Tales for the Holy Season,* isn't a devotional reader, strictly speaking. Yet for young families especially, this anthology of short stories can make a cherished companion in the weeks preceding Easter and during the holiday itself. Some of these stories are perennial childhood favorites that come alive when read aloud to the whole family, such as Oscar Wilde's "The Selfish Giant." Others are classic works of literature for teenagers and adults, including selections by Leo Tolstoy, Anton Chekhov, C. S. Lewis, and Elizabeth Goudge. Either way, what unites the stories in this illustrated volume is a tenderness and reverence for the mystery of death and resurrection that strikes the heart anew each year. ⬎

Michael and Margaretha Sattler

JASON LANDSEL

IN MARCH OF 1525, a young couple new to Zurich found themselves in what would prove to be a dangerous Bible study. The group of Christians had started meeting only two months before to discuss the ideas of the Reformation. They sought to return to the simplicity of the early church, and became convinced that baptism was something that only adult believers should undertake. And so, that spring, Michael Sattler was baptized as an adult – a crime under both civil and church law, punishable with death. He and his wife, Margaretha, were now part of the new movement of "re-baptizers," or Anabaptists.

Born in southern Germany around 1490, Michael had entered a Benedictine monastery near Freiburg, where he had served as prior; Margaretha had been a Beguine. They had both encountered the ideas of the Reformers, and each found in the other a partner eager to follow Christ with their whole lives.

In Zurich, Michael quickly became a leader in the Anabaptist group. When it was disbanded, the couple was expelled from the city. Seeking to preserve this community of revival, Michael met with Martin Bucer and other mainstream Reformation leaders. But the Sattlers' uncompromising stance went too far for the more cautious reformers.

More and more people sought to enter illegal Anabaptist communities. But they were scattered and hidden. Finally, in February 1527, Michael presided over a gathering of radical leaders. Here, they drafted what would come to be called the Schleitheim Confession, after the Swiss town where they met. It outlined the fundamental principles of their movement, based on the Sermon on the Mount. These included voluntary baptism for believers only, with no compulsion in religion; nonviolence; and mutual accountability in the church.

When the Sattlers returned home from this meeting, they were almost immediately captured by Austrian forces. In addition to the charge of Anabaptism, Sattler was accused of being a traitor for opposing war against the Ottoman Turks:

> If the Turks should come, we ought not to resist them. For it is written [Matt. 5:21]: Thou shalt not kill. We must [rather] beseech God with earnest prayer to repel and resist them. . . . If warring were right, I would rather take the field against so-called Christians who persecute, capture, and kill pious Christians than against the Turks [who] know nothing of the Christian faith.

As the trial began, the Archduke deployed soldiers for fear of an uprising.

Five days later, on May 20, 1527, Michael Sattler was tortured and burned alive. On his way to the execution site he called on the crowds to repent, and prayed for the judges. Eight days after her husband's death, Margaretha was drowned in the River Neckar. She said she would have rather gone to the fire with her husband.

"Almighty, eternal God," Sattler prayed as he was bound to the stake, "Thou art the way and the truth; because I have not been shown to be in error, I will with thy help on this day testify to the truth and seal it with my blood." ↘

Jason Landsel is the artist for Plough's *"Forerunners" series, including the painting opposite.*